C0064 42853

This bo
be rene
date, a

D1356081

Written with Tom Sykes

Quercus

To my darling, long-suffering wife Janie, my amazing boys Charlie and Tom and my feral hound Jelly Bean

First published in Great Britain in 2018 by Quercus.

Quercus Editions Ltd
Carmelite House
50 Victoria Embankment
London EC4Y 0DZ

An Hachette UK company

Copyright © Henry Cole 2018

The moral right of Henry Cole to
be identified as the author of this work has been
asserted in accordance with the Copyright,
Designs and Patents Act, 1988.

All rights reserved. No part of this publication
may be reproduced or transmitted in any form
or by any means, electronic or mechanical,
including photocopy, recording, or any
information storage and retrieval system,
without permission in writing from the publisher.

A CIP catalogue record for this book is available
from the British Library

HB ISBN 978 1 78747 104 7
TPB ISBN 978 1 78747 108 5
Ebook ISBN 978 1 78747 106 1

Every effort has been made to contact copyright holders.
However, the publishers will be glad to rectify in future
editions any inadvertent omissions brought to their attention.

Quercus Editions Ltd hereby exclude all liability to the extent
permitted by law for any errors or omissions in this book and for any loss,
damage or expense (whether direct or indirect) suffered by a
third party relying on any information contained in this book.

All images courtesy of Henry Cole

10 9 8 7 6 5 4 3 2 1

Typeset by CC Book Production
Printed and bound in Great Britain by Clays Ltd, Elcograf S.p.A.

Contents

Prologue

It's a cracking summer morning in 1987, I'm twenty-three and I'm wanging it out of town on the A3 in my racing leathers.

Everything in my life is going down the shitter – I'm addicted to heroin, the business is fucked, the girlfriend has left me, the flat is about to be repossessed. But who cares?

It's one of those perfect days to be on a bike.

I am behaving myself as best as I can, but somewhere near Oxshott, the A3 goes into three lanes.

I open her up, and now I'm really pinning it.

The traffic parts, like the Red Sea for Moses, and the outside lane stretches out in front of me, shining and empty.

Irresistible.

So.

Here we go.

Twist.

120.

Beautiful.

I've got the race pipe on and I'm making plenty of noise.

Twist.

125.

Tucked perfectly into the fairing. I can hear the wind whistling past my helmet. All that shit – the flat, Billy, Tonya, the business – it's all gone from my mind.

Twist.

130.

This is exactly what this beautiful, long, peeling bend was made for.

I'm cranked over on the left-hand side. Truly alive. Truly here.

Motorcyclists have never needed a mindfulness coach to tell us it's all about the journey.

Life's good, man.

Too good.

Because as I come round the corner, there's a massive Alsatian, standing in the middle of the fast lane, staring right at me.

I swerve to avoid it, but grab too much front brake, and now I'm going down like a sack of shit on the A3.

Just like everyone said, the world is going into slow motion.

Plenty of time for contemplation.

First set of wheels!

Chapter 1

I can't think of anywhere in the world I'd rather be than on a motorbike.

And I can't think of anywhere in the world I'd less like to be than in a car.

What does the car driver have? A tin frigging box, that's what.

When you're driving a car, you're not taking part; you're a spectator. You're in a poxy metal can. If it's cold, you turn up the heating; if you're hungry, you chew a wine gum.

If you fart, you wind down the window.

You might be looking at what's going on, but you're definitely not a part of it.

When you're riding a motorbike, you *are* the landscape. You're looking after your needs, and you're appreciating the simple things.

'I've just gone down into this valley; it's a little bit warmer. Is that rain? No. But it's raining over there. Result. It's not going to rain on my road.'

When you sit on a motorbike, as I have done for tens of thousands of miles all over the world, you're on your own.

I firmly believe that every single person who rides a motorbike yearns to be an individual. But society dictates that individuality is bred out of us from a very early age these days.

It's much easier for the various establishments that run the planet (that used to mean the Church, but now it means Facebook and Google) if people don't do too much thinking for themselves. Stick them in a car and they're a number. Stick us on a bike and we are who we want to be.

Me and my first horse power: Honey the pony!

Chapter 2

Motorcycling is the last great refuge of the individual. Take my Uncle Redbeard, for example.

I first met Dick Redbeard when my father decided it was about time we went to see the relatives before they croaked.

So Mum, Dad and I hiked off in our grey Morris van with me, aged eight, rolling around in the back on a mattress – the health-and-safety child seat of the 1960s.

Driving up to Liverpool on the A-roads from Norfolk, where we lived in an isolated, old rectory, was extremely boring. As an only child, I had to make my own fun. On this occasion I passed the time by bringing the Lego steering wheel I had built, and using it to steer along with the old man.

My dad spent the whole drive up telling my mother and me how mad Redbeard was: 'The man's a raving loon,' he said. 'Rich as Croesus, but he gave up drinking Guinness when the price rose above a shilling a bottle. No idea about modern life, none whatsoever.'

My dad seemed blissfully unaware that although Redbeard was actually my mum's relative, he might as well have been describing himself: they were peas in a pod.

Dad wore a three-piece tweed suit every day of his life. He loathed and feared the modern world in all its incarnations, which was the reason why I never went abroad, wore jeans or ate pasta until I was fifteen.

We finally arrived at Uncle Dick Redbeard's house – a large Edwardian pile set apart from the other houses around it by its storybook shabbiness. I doubt he'd ever spent a penny on it, and I guarantee he would never once have spoken to his neighbours. I don't think he would have known what that word meant.

I remember the smell of that house more than anything else: musk and leather and a certain sort of distinct oldness.

Redbeard himself was clearly every bit as bonkers as my dad had said. He was old and weak and he offered sherry to my parents and diddly-squit to me, as was the way of people of that ilk and era when they saw a child. The adults stood around talking in the drawing room, so I went out into the garden to play. I don't know how long I had been messing around out there when Redbeard stuck his head out of this crazy corrugated iron shed attached to the back of the house and called me over in his very posh voice: 'Come and have a look in here.'

This was my very first experience of a proper shed. It was stuffed to the gills with old motorbikes. And in the movie version of my life, this is when the angels descend, playing their little harps.

I gazed across the sea of leather and chrome.

'What are they all doing in here?' I asked, wide-eyed.

'Well, I can't get rid of them, but I'm too old to ride them now,' he said, wistfully.

'So they stay in here?'

He nodded. 'This one's a Triumph,' he said, pointing at one bike. Then, indicating another, 'This is a BSA.'

I had no idea what these words meant, but I knew from his reverent tone that they were hugely, massively important. And I also knew I was being invited to experience something special and deeply personal in Redbeard's world.

I ran my hands over the gleaming motorbikes, smelling the oil, breathing it all in.

Bolted onto the handlebars of one of the bikes was a bronze dragon.

Redbeard saw me staring at it and said, 'That used to be a car mascot. I put it on the bike.'

My father and Redbeard were aristocratic eccentrics to a man. But whereas my father preferred to reject modernity by hiding away in his large house and telling everyone who came by to fuck off, Redbeard was actually able to escape the pressures of social acceptability through his obsession with motorcycles.

Even then, I loved the fact he wasn't afraid to be different.

That was what struck a chord with me.

That was what I spent the next forty years trying to be.

Different.

Chapter 3

On the way back home, all I could talk about were the bikes.

I wanted one.

My father was dead-set against it from the first moment: 'Why do you want a blasted motorbike? Men with beards ride them, and they smell and steal things,' was one of his classic comments on the issue.

But it made no difference what he said. I was hooked from that first moment in Redbeard's shed. From then on, a motorbike was all I ever really wanted, and the more my father said I wasn't having one, the more I yearned for one.

A few years later, Redbeard died. And by the time we got up to his house, all the bikes had gone. Other members of the family had gone in and snaffled the lot.

This was totally, utterly devastating to me because Redbeard's shed had loomed large in my imaginary life, and I had always banked on getting one of those bikes. Now my big chance had gone. Vanished.

I did, however, get a pair of his goggles.

Redbeard's goggles became my prized possession. I used to wear them on my bicycle, a Grifter, which I had kitted out with battery-powered twin headlights and indicators – my first ever custom build.

I'd ride round and round the woods in Norfolk, dreaming of being on a motorbike, wearing a baseball hat on my head, a scarf over my nose and Uncle Dick Redbeard's goggles over my eyes.

When I was ten or eleven, I discovered *Motorcycle News*, or *MCN*, as it is better known. I would cycle down to the village shop to buy it. These trips were almost my only direct contact with the 'real' world and, thanks to the seclusion in which I was being reared, I was utterly baffled by it.

I'd walk into the shop and the lady behind the counter would say, 'Busy?' which is local speak for, 'How are you doing?'

I would stare blankly at her, feeling so foolish – as if I'd done something wrong – with absolutely no idea what she meant.

Sometimes I'd think she was talking to someone behind me, and I'd turn round to check.

Nope. No one there.

So I'd get my pennies together as quick as I could, grab *MCN* and get out of there.

I just didn't understand the outside world. Which isn't surprising.

I was born into a fairly privileged, upper middle-class background, deliberately kept away from anything vaguely approaching normal life.

The Victorian rectory we lived in, up in Norfolk, was in the middle of nowhere. It had fourteen bedrooms. And who lived there? Me, my mum, my former-army-major, eccentric old man and a dog called Lulu. The only thing my dad basically knew how to do was to kill someone, and all my mum knew was how to be his unpaid servant. She spoke like a divinely stoic 1950s' BBC continuity announcer. She has always been my rock.

I was sent to Beeston Hall, a private boarding school up on the north Norfolk coast. Like home, this was also totally segregated from modern society. You never had anyone coming to give a talk on rock and roll or whatever the kids get these days. We just played British Bulldog all day, which our parents thought was perfect.

I never really had any friends over during the holidays because it would take three hours to go and collect someone in the Morris van. So if anyone did come, they would have to stay for a week.

It was odd.

During the summer holidays at breakfast my father would say, 'What are you up to today?'

I'd go, 'Er, I don't know.'

'I'll tell you what you're going to do. You're going to fuck off after breakfast, and then you're going to come back in at lunch. Then you're going to have lunch and fuck off again and come back at supper. I don't want you in the house. I want you out and about playing in the woods.'

He had every good intention, but this didn't really work out very well for me.

Vintage 1890s Petrol and Oil Dispenser

The key difference between someone who is in trouble with their collecting habit and someone who's got it under control is how they look after their stuff.

This is my pride and joy: one of the first ever petrol dispensers. They were in chemists in the 1890s. You'd go in and you'd say, 'I'll have a quart of petrol, my fine fellow.' They'd set the lever to 'QUART' and, it would dispense precisely that amount. It works perfectly, because, for me, collecting is also about preserving.

Collectors are all curators. The minute you lose sight of that as a collector, then you are doing our history a disservice.

That pump was rotting when I got it. And I've restored it. I even got the right colours. But if I was to cut the top off, right, and bolt a glass sheet on top and turn it into a coffee table for kitting out a massive urban flat, I'd be an arsehole, because a very rare petrol dispenser has then been lost.

If I customize a bike, I only customize one that there are plenty of. Or I'll build one myself, so hopefully, one day, it might be part of that history. But to brutalize something – something that is rare – is unforgivable in my view.

I'm not a person who wants to just stack up stuff. Whatever I have, it's got to be mint and it's got to be beautiful.

So why do I collect all this stuff? I don't really know. I don't particularly want to use it just to show off, like a Lamborghini; but I do love showing it to people I like and respect who are interested. Other shed people, basically.

I just want to say, 'Look at this petrol pump. Don't you love that? They used to have them in the chemists.'

It gives me great pleasure to tell my fellow shed people that.

Chapter 4

Those trips down to the village on my Grifter were my only excursions out of a very privileged but confined existence, and *Motorcycle News* became my window into what I thought was the real world – a world largely populated by crazy nutbars, by the looks of things, with greasy hair and fags hanging out of their mouths, dirty and covered in oil.

Barry Sheene was the big star.

Life, as represented by *Motorcycle News*, looked amazing. You could grow your hair. You didn't have to wash. You could smoke and swear and wear leathers and tell everyone to fuck off.

For an insecure, isolated little boy with a side parting, growing up in a remote vicarage with an eccentric father and a tremulous mother, it was a revelation.

MCN whispered to me, 'There is another way, Henry!'

The guys in *MCN* didn't give a damn about tweed jackets and good manners. These guys were obviously dangerous. They were the kind of people I was being brought up to avoid at all costs.

It was an alluring, exciting world, and I wanted to be in it.

All I needed was a bike.

My obsession with motorbikes grew and grew. But it wasn't until I was about twelve, by which time my parents had moved to Winchester, that I got to sit on one for the first time.

The fact that this momentous event happened after we moved is significant. One of the great things about living in a town was the proximity of *other people*.

I actually managed to make a friend – Tom, whose parents ran a kind of old folks' home with bungalows dotted everywhere, and tarmac roads connecting them.

Anyway, I was over at Tom's one day and he opened up the garage and there was a blue Honda CB250 RSA single. He said, 'You like motorbikes, Henry. Why don't you have a go on that?'

Now, of course, there was no one there to help, to show me what to do. It wasn't as if Tom had ever gone on it. It was just in his garage. He'd only looked at it. I think it belonged to a friend of his father.

And I didn't have the first clue how to ride it.

But that wasn't going to stop me.

I'd been pedalling on the Grifter for the last eight years, imagining I was going to get on a motorcycle, and now, that amazing day had come.

This was my big chance. So I laid my hands on the handlebars of this enormous motorcycle that I could hardly push, and I wheeled it out of the garage.

And in that moment, something happened. I became one of those people in *Motorcycle News*. I felt different, somehow. Empowered.

Just like that. I was in the club.

There was this network of tarmac paths in front of me, and I just thought, This is it; this is the place to do it. I'm going to get on this bike, ride it, and my life is never, ever going to be same again.

I got on.

And suddenly, all my confidence, all my joy – it all vanished, vaporized, disappeared, and I was just completely and utterly terrified. I'd been dreaming about this moment for half of my life, but now that it was a reality . . . well . . . I'd never really thought about reality in my dreams or my imagination.

Specifically, I'd never thought about how you actually rode one of these things.

I know now that it must have been left in neutral, or else I'd never have been able to wheel it out of the garage. So when I started it up by pressing the button, and heard that engine growl, my confidence returned. I'd done that!

But how was I going to get it to move?

Tom said, 'I think you pull that thing, and press that thing in you know, and then let it out really slowly.'

So I gingerly pulled what I now know is the clutch lever, and pressed the gear shift down with my left foot, and then I released the clutch and VROOOM, I tore off down the path, totally out of control, no clue how to stop, no idea what I was doing, bunny hopping all the way. I left the tarmac, veered up onto the grass, careened into a bush and the thing came to a stop.

In the space of five, maybe ten seconds, my dreams had turned to tatters. The future I'd longed for for so many years had turned out to be a complete nightmare. All those fantasies – how I was going to be dangerous and ride off and fuck society and show my old man what I was made of and beat Barry Sheene – they were all gone.

I was just devastated.

Pushing that motorbike back into the garage and bicycling home from Tom's place, I was totally bereft. I didn't understand how reality could be so harsh.

Now, all these years later, I look back on it and I think, Actually Henry, mate, you did all right. You kept it shiny side up and you stayed on. You must have got it back into neutral or you wouldn't have been able to get it back in the garage. You survived it.

A few months later I had another go.

This time, I was on a suitable bike for a first timer, a little yellow Honda Melody, no gears, with a basket on the front. Same place, Tom's gaff, same little roads. I don't know who it belonged to this time; a sister or a cousin of Tom's or something. It was definitely a female's bike.

It was twist and go. And I got on it and off I went!

I could ride!

I could ride, man!

I went round and round that complex on this yellow thing with a basket and that feeling came back – that feeling that I know now a free spirit gets every time he or she gets on a bike, even a little Honda Melody with a shopping basket on the front.

For me, it was an amazing moment because that's when I realized that my dream could become a reality.

I didn't learn properly how to ride a bike with a clutch and gears until I was about fourteen. There was this guy called Harvey who was a photocopier salesman and he looked like a cross between Noel Edmonds on a bad day and the Bay City Rollers – but so did a lot of people back then.

He drove a massive brown Cortina estate that he used to take his photocopiers around in (because they were so big in those days), but he also had an RD250 Yamaha that he let me have a go on whenever I wanted.

Looking back on it, maybe it was weird that I was hanging around with this older dude, but I've never been someone who has been bothered about people's ages. He was just part of our gang.

I got the hang of it pretty quick, because I understood the main thing was that you have to accelerate as you let the clutch out, and that's when it all started to make sense.

Harvey had another bike as well – a Z650 – and so off we went down the road together. Totally illegal, of course, and I've no idea why he let me ride it, but, hey, would Barry Sheene have cared about a little detail like that?

Harvey told me not to do anything in a hurry, and I think that's still the most valuable advice about riding motorbikes that anyone has ever given me. I still keep to that adage today, especially in the rain.

I'd ride whenever I could with Harvey, and it was a watershed time: as soon as I started riding that bike, that's when life became interesting, as far as I was concerned.

By the time I was about fourteen, I'd sorted it out, you know. I didn't do my test till I was eighteen. Nowadays, the test is a huge, convoluted experience that costs about

£750, with people wearing headphones and hi-viz jackets following you and talking to you just like you're in a car with them. In my day, you'd take your RD250 (although I hired a bike for the day) up to Merton, in London, and drive round four sides of a square, while a geezer stood on the corner and said, 'Right, next time you come round, I'm going to step out for an emergency stop'.

Well, he stepped out 50 yards away from me. I pulled up and thought I'd better go a little bit further and brake, otherwise that's embarrassing. My mate Chas Smash, he actually fell off doing his test and he still passed. He got back on the bike and came round and said, 'Everything all right?'

Yeah, fine, absolutely sweet, mate, no stress. And he passed even though he had a gravel rash on his knee.

Chapter 5

So as you can maybe guess, I really yearned as a kid to have an off-road motocross bike, you know, and throw myself at the countryside. But my father was having none of that. He totally and utterly loathed my obsession with motorbikes. And I'm absolutely convinced that if he had taken me off to be taught properly in a safe environment like kids do nowadays, I wouldn't be as fanatical as I am now.

Fortunately for my father (or perhaps, unfortunately, as it turned out) he had unlimited faith in Britain's private school system, and he was unshakeably confident that all the motorbike nonsense would be knocked out of my head at Eton.

I had never been involved in any discussion about where I was going to school. It was always going to be Eton. In fact, I think my father's exact words were: 'It's either Eton or nothing. It's up to you.'

So, Eton, then.

My father was educated in the Raj in India, but my mother's family had been going to Eton since at least 1821, when my great-great-great-great uncle William Ewart Gladstone, later Prime Minister Gladstone, rocked up for his first day.

If you want to go to Eton these days, you have to do about six million tests to make sure you are super intelligent, but in those days, the system was a bit more relaxed.

I was prepped to take common entrance in the summer like everybody else, and then I was going to start at Eton in September. But one day, during the Easter term, Swindells (Beeston Hall's headmaster) appeared and said: 'Cole, come to my study.' I, naturally enough, thought, Fuck, I'm going to get beaten again. But in I went and he said, 'Right, I've just had a call from Eton, there's a space available now, so you're taking common entrance in two weeks and you'll be going to Eton in the summer term.'

'Er, what? Ok . . .'

I guess some rogue kids had got expelled or something, and Swindell figured I had a better chance of getting in if I went for it off-season.

I can't remember taking the exam, but I do remember the interview.

I sat down opposite this bloke called McCrum and he said, 'So, on your mother's side, there's been a whole lineage of Gladstones here, hasn't there, Henry?'

'Yes, sir.'

'Do you play cricket?'

'Yes, sir. I'm in the first XI' (which it was pretty difficult not to be at my prep school).

'Do you open the batting, Cole?'

'Well, I have done, sir, yes.'

'Good, good. Well, see you in the summer!'

'Ok, sir. Thank you, sir.'

And so that summer, off I went. There were eighteen of us who went to Eton in the summer term – the summer half, as they call it – and then, at the end of term, we stayed down a year when all the people we'd got to know went up.

It was madness.

Mavis

Meet Mavis, my Norton ES2. My daily ride.

I found her in a shed. Like all good things she's a mongrel. She's a mismatch of everything. I cannot tell you which bit of Mavis should be on which bike. All I do know is that whoever built her got it right.

She's an old Norton 500, with an ES2 engine and a doll's head gearbox, and I got her for *Shed and Buried*.

I got on her for the first time, kicked her and she sparked into life on that first kick, after being in a shed for five years.

I filled up the tyres with air and I rode her from that moment on.

Once I'd fettled her a bit, I did something very stupid. I sold her to my mate Dave for two thousand two hundred quid. I couldn't sleep that night, and the next morning I rang Dave up and said, 'Mate, I'm sorry to fuck you about. I've got to buy her back.'

She's from 1947 and she is the most mellow, laid-back, glorious, single-cylinder motorcycle you will ever ride.

Whoever built her just got it right, in the riding position, the styling and stance of her and her ability to calm the soul as you're riding along.

She just fuds along, and I have never, ever even taken the engine apart because I think to myself, If she goes this well, why bother changing it?

She is in no way ostentatious. She in no way offends anyone. She's got an endearing, rather feminine quality about her.

Mave should have girder forks, but she has telescopic forks, and it kind of works. I worry if you tried to return it to standard, you'd wreck the whole feel of her and the reason for her being special. She's like me: a mismatch. I'm just a load of parts that shouldn't work properly, but I seem to get on with life. And so does she.

She's everything I want from a motorcycle at my age, for road riding, which means she's predictable, she's mellow, she'll bumble along at 60 all day long on country roads and she's understated. She's classless and timeless, in my view, and living proof of the fact that in motorcycling, the amount of money you spend on a bike is irrelevant.

Chapter 6

So there I was at Eton. And after my weird childhood, it all seemed very normal. I fitted in pretty well.

I made a lifelong friend in those first few weeks – a guy called Charlie Meynell. We were absolutely chalk and cheese, completely, and still are to this day. He wore tweed and I smoked weed. If he sees a bloke on a bike, he assumes they're about to kill him.

There were no longer cold baths in the mornings at Eton in the 1970s, but there was still morning school, where you had to get up and go to a lesson before breakfast. And they still had a system called fagging – and no, it wasn't what the word 'fag' and public school might get some people thinking. Being someone's fag meant you were their personal slave: you had to polish their shoes and all that kind of stuff. The fag masters were in the top year, and the fags were in the bottom year.

Eton was a hundred per cent boarding school, and the students were divided up across twenty-five boarding houses, dotted around the town. I was a fag to this very nice geezer called Lord Balniel. Now of course, I'd heard all the stories and I'd watched *Tom Brown's School Days*, and I was terrified that Flashman was going to come and bugger me or I was going to be sexually abused. But I've got to say, it was a very positive experience – and fair play to old Lord Balniel. I'll never forget: I turn up the first day to his room (because we all had separate rooms) and he goes, 'Right, what I want is my socks cleaned and I want my shirts done; you'll find my rugby boots there, you need to clean those,' and all that kind of stuff.

So I was kind of set these rules by Ant – as I called Lord Balniel, after a while – and it was fine. And all these well-meaning people who say how wrong it is to have a school system where one boy is allowed to boss around another just because he is older than him – what they don't understand is that I would never have talked to Lord Balniel if I hadn't been his fag because he was up at the top of the school; he was a prefect, and he wore a fancy waistcoat and a special tie. But actually, he treated me brilliantly and he included me in stuff that he was up to.

He'd say, 'Right, Cole, this afternoon you'll come and support me on the First XV,' or whatever it was.

'Ok, guv,' I'd say, and I'd go and I'd watch. It made me feel part of the school – and it was the first time I'd really felt part of anything.

The thing that never sat right with me about Eton was the feeling of elitism. While I knew that by virtue of being there, I was part of the elite, I thought, through the pages of *Motorcycle News*, that there was more fun to be had being a regular geezer. But then I didn't really know what a regular geezer was. Genuinely – I'd never even worn a pair of jeans.

My first rebellion was smoking. That was probably where I started to slightly go off the rails at Eton.

I'd smoked occasional cigarettes since the age of eight, because at that age, I was desperate to try it and my father gave me a black Russian Sobranie cigarette with a gold tip. He said, 'If you really want to smoke so much, then smoke this.'

I think he was hoping I'd be sick or something, but I wasn't. I smoked that fag right down to the butt, and said to my father, 'Can I have another?'

He went, 'Right, this is the deal. You can have a cigarette on Christmas Day every year and that's it.'

By the age of thirteen, I was allowed one cigarette a week, and I was inhaling by then.

At Eton, I started smoking fags profusely, and I loved the sense of rebellion and belonging that came with that.

To this day, I've never thrown a party because I'm terrified that no one will turn up. Letting people know they were invited to come to my room and smoke fags is the closest I ever got. My room was the best for smoking because it had a kind of ventilation shaft in the wall that literally sucked all the cigarette smoke out of the airspace.

I became part of a clan. Even then, I had a knack that when I went to a party, I could find people like me. I could pick them out immediately. It wasn't just that their shirts were hanging out or their hair was messy. I could tell that, deep down, they were the same as me: rebels without a cause, rebelling against something that they didn't even understand. It was only much, much later that I found out that those people I could spot a mile off were all addicts.

What happened to really kick things off was what happened to a lot of people my age – punk.

Just because we were locked away in some posh boarding school, don't think punk didn't have the same mind-blowing effect on us that it had on so many other teenagers in 1977 and 78.

We loved the idea of anarchy as much as anyone. There was an energy at school that the system couldn't contain – a sense that the kids were revolting, rebelling against all this poshery that they had been immersed in.

I'll never forget when 'Eton Rifles' by The Jam came out. It was, of course, a song about class war, and how unfairly the system was stacked in favour of privileged Etonians like us. There certainly was no shortage of twats who would have jeered and spat at an unemployment march, but there was also a ton of us who were as sick of the privilege of Eton as Paul Weller himself.

It was partly that song that got me into music. I took up drumming (really badly), having originally started off playing the bass guitar (really, really badly). I got a band together with my cousin Charlie Gladstone; I played drums and he sang and this other guy, Nick, was on guitar.

We decided we were going to go on tour, and our first gig, which we somehow persuaded our music teacher to organize for us, was at a local girls' school. I bought pink, fluffy bondage trousers and a UK Subs T-shirt, and I thought I was the bomb. Charlie was more into two-tone stuff, black and white checked trousers and that. We were a complete mishmash of different styles, but that was what was great about music then – everything was a jumble of all kinds of looks and genres and that was the fun of it; everyone was exploring everything.

Chapter 7

As I was in a band, I felt it was incumbent upon me to smoke dope. I used to smoke weed down at the school's music studios. And I would deal it, going up to Slough to buy it in bulk, selling a bit to pay for my own.

Then, like a million other tokers before us, we had a bright idea: it's a plant, right? Why not grow it ourselves? Save the hassle of going into Slough.

It was not a professional operation. I grew the plants in my window box (well, *attempted* to grow would be a fairer description of my horticultural endeavours). Smart, eh? Obviously, my housemaster, Mr Roynon, found it. It was quite a big deal and it triggered a schoolwide drugs purge. They got the police dog in to have a sniff about. Six of my mates got expelled in the fallout.

I thought, This is it. They're going to kick me out. The old man's not going to be happy at all. I said to Nick, 'We're stuffed, mate. They've kicked out six of us and we're the last. So here's what we're going to do, man, we're just going to tell the truth.'

He looked at me like I was mad, but what else could we do?

I went into the headmaster first. He said, 'Henry, you've been caught twelve times for smoking cigarettes, and now you're smoking this stuff? Why?'

I explained that Nick and I thought we were cool (true), and we were in a rock-and-roll band (true) and we'd tried smoking a bit of weed (true) – but we didn't really like it (sort of true) and we hadn't smoked it for a couple of weeks (not at all true).

'But you've been growing it, Henry,' he said.

'Well, I've been trying, sir, but nothing's happened, really. I mean, we got some shoots [which they'd found], but nothing more than that, really. I can only apologise, sir. It's just been me and Nick having a quick try, and I guess you've got to try things in life, haven't you, sir?'

He looked at me strangely and sent me out to wait in the corridor. I was convinced we were finished.

But Nick went in and said the same thing, and when he called us both back in, he said, 'I've expelled everyone else who's been involved. But you two have told the truth and that's different to the other six, so I'm going to rusticate both of you for four weeks. You're to go home and revise. Go and see your housemaster and tell him you need to be on a train, now.'

I got changed out of my school clothes and Roynon drove me to the train station in my bondage trousers and my mother's black rubber macintosh. I'd also shaved off all my hair and had a skinhead. So when I got to Winchester train station, my mother didn't recognise me. Not surprising, really, as when I had left for school at the end of the holidays I was wearing brogues, corduroy trousers, a tweed jacket and my hair was in a side parting.

Six weeks is a long time when you're sixteen.

Eventually, she identified me. She burst into tears, as we got into her little Triumph Dolomite.

We got home, walked in the door and my father looked at me. He said, 'You fucking cunt.'

I said, 'I'm so sorry, Father, I didn't mean to . . .'

He said, 'I don't give a fuck about the drugs. What do you look like?'

'I'm trying to be cool, Dad, you know?'

'Cool? You look like a twat! Get out of your mother's fucking gardening coat.'

Lots of bikers have issues with drugs. From those first days smoking weed at school, I became one of them.

Blimey, I haven't had a drink or drug for thirty years! It's taken me that long to realize that motorcycling and addiction were two responses – one healthy and one unhealthy – to the same thing: the feeling I had that everyone was always dissatisfied with me, that I didn't fit in somehow. I desperately wanted to be an individual but I didn't have a bloody clue how or why.

Métisse Desert Racer

My Métisse Desert Racer is a Steve McQueen desert racer replica. It's a replica of the bike he used to race in the deserts of America. Well, I say it's a replica, but it's still made by the same company, so technically a continuation is what it is, really.

The Rickman brothers under the name Rickman Métisse were the first people to design a frame specifically for off-road use back in the 60s. And Bud Ekins, who was Steve McQueen's hero, had a Triumph shop in Sherman Oaks in Los Angeles and he imported the first Rickman frames. Steve saw them, and specced out one with the exact replica components that I've got on mine.

That bike is made by Métisse to this day, and it's an utterly unbelievable vehicle. Now, I stupidly took it to South Africa and it didn't make it, but that was my own fault because I hadn't specced it properly. But then I rode it through the Balkans and it didn't miss a beat.

I ride it like mad today. If I've got to go somewhere, I'll either take Mavis (my Norton) or this Steve McQueen replica. It's the most wonderful thing. It makes such a great noise. It handles so well and what I love about it is that I'm going on-road to a meet or something like that, and a car comes the other way down a narrow lane, and, hey, I go off on the verge, you know. It's just great. I wait for these cars to come, so I've got every excuse to do a bit of off-roading as I carry on my way. Anyone who looks at it would say that embodies the 60s. It's the coolest sled ever.

Chapter 8

Filling my days while I was suspended was no problem. Back in 1978–9, Winchester was very much a provincial town, but people were just beginning to commute from there to London because the train service was good, so the Audi-driving middle class was quietly infiltrating.

There was a secretarial college, and a couple of schools, so it was a rich target for chicks. I was part of a group of wasters, some public-school kids and some locals, and we used to spend our school holidays hanging out on the Buttercross, a monument in the precinct. I'd be in my Harringtons, with a skinhead, and I'd just sit there and wait for chicks.

Me and my mate Alan – he had black hair and a long black overcoat – we used to stay out all night just for the sake of it.

Alan had a friend called Dean who worked in the Baker's Oven overnight, and we'd go in and eat sausage rolls in the early hours.

We took a loaf of bread off Dean one night and started kicking it around the precinct. I punted it and it went way up in the air, landing on the International Stores' roof.

As it was rolling down, two policemen came round the corner. One of them said, 'Oi, you two, what are you doing, loafing around?' And as he said it, the loaf hit the ground in front of them.

This was one of the highlights of my teenage years.

So you get the picture: Winchester was a pretty quiet place, but we did our best to make our own fun. We went to each other's houses, smoked fags, threw parties, all that kind of thing.

And when we were sixteen, some of us got bikes, little 50ccs at first – mopeds, basically – then bigger ones, so we could bomb around and go places. We'd ride our bikes from Winchester to Hursley to Whitchurch. I was one of the younger ones in the crowd, so, although I'd do a bit of illegal riding if Harvey or one of the other guys would let me, I'd usually be on the back of my mate Guy's CB550K3.

We used to hang out at Mr Pipkin's Wine Bar – that's where it rocked, man – and Alice's restaurant next door was a burger joint I used to work in. We thought we were the cool kids. And a big part of our culture was smoking dope.

But I slowly realized that was the part I hated. The stuff we were scoring now was so much stronger than the gear at school and it made me feel like I was wired up to the wrong Mars bar. Smoking dope became like bungee jumping. You get quite excited before you do it – 'I'm going to go and get wrecked with a few mates': that's the bit where you are walking out onto the bridge. Then you're rolling this joint the length of an album cover, that takes about forty minutes with all these people telling tall stories about how they hot-knifed an ounce and how they had the world's biggest bong: that's like tying on the elastic round your feet. Then you spark it up: that's like when you actually jump.

It's one of the most awful experiences known to man.

Maybe it was because I had some innate insecurity, but smoking dope induced ultimate paranoia in me. I'd sit there, in a kind of catatonic state, waiting to feel scared and then, sure enough, I'd feel scared; terrified, really uncomfortable.

'Did I smile too much then? Did that guy smile back at me? Why? Why not? Hey, that guy didn't pass me the joint! Does he hate me?' And then, inevitably, I'd have too much – like a bong or something – and I'd feel sick, pull a whitey and the room would be spinning and I couldn't walk.

Grass was slightly different because at least with grass there was uncontrollable laughter, so that was fun for a bit.

But it was generally just a miserable experience.

It was through drugs that I met Guy and the fifteen other people he was kind of hanging out with. They all wore black and rode motorbikes. One day, they all came round to my house and I was in – suddenly, I was a part of this clan of people who wore black cowboy boots and black jeans and black T-shirts and were into Genesis and The Sound and Tom Petty.

And they produced this thing, a bong. I had a hoof on this and I didn't know whether it was New York or New Year. And then they went home.

I went to bed.

I was just a mess after that first bong. I couldn't get up for a day. It was horrendous, but these guys were rebels like me, and part of being in their gang was smoking weed. That was what the cool people were doing. I think that's why a lot of people take drugs; because they think it's cool.

They want to be part of the gang. And that insecurity, that actually is the nucleus of addiction; that's it, right there.

A lot of sober addicts will tell you the same thing – drug addiction is not about taking drugs. Drugs are only the symptom of addiction.

It's about this void inside.

I had that void from a very early age, and I had tried a million things to fill it.

I was from a ridiculously privileged background. I was spoiled rotten. Ok, my father was a complete eccentric, but my childhood was a safe place to be. He never came close to hitting me, and although he never said he loved me, it was obvious he did.

But I just felt so empty all the time.

Out of the fifteen of us back then – Guy, his mates and me – nine are dead now; I am one of the lucky ones.

Chapter 9

When I went back to school for my final year after being suspended for drugs, I thought I was cooler than ever.

By complete luck, in that year, the school tried a radical experiment; they invited sixteen girls into the sixth form. They were mainly the school masters' daughters, or the daughters of former masters.

There was this one gorgeous bird. We were all obsessed with her. She used to come to my room to smoke – everyone did, so there was a queue outside my room half the time – and one day, wow, we ended up in bed together.

I got laid.

Anyway, afterwards, I'm lying there naked, and we're both smoking at the ventilator, talking shit, shooting the breeze after a shag, feeling pretty damned cool. And Roynon comes straight in.

I'm starkers.

She's starkers.

Bedclothes everywhere. Knickers on the floor.

And he says, 'Cole! Smoking! Down to my office, now!' and marches out again.

I got eight hours of moss picking – for the smoking. The naked girl was never mentioned.

*

I got suspended for the last time at the very end of my school career, when I got caught smoking fags, again.

'Henry, your housemaster says he has found two bin liners full of empty cigarette packets in your room,' sighed the headmaster. 'Go home. Just go home, and come back for the exams.'

My father went ballistic that last time. 'You always were a wrong 'un!' I remember him yelling at me.

'But Dad, I want to be a musician—'

'A musician? What's the end game?' he shouted. 'Playing for Leo Sayer on Terry fucking Wogan?'

There's not much you can say to that, is there?

The Quartermaster Drag Bike

This is a drag bike from the 1960s. Found it in a shed.

It's called the Quartermaster because it was owned by an army gentleman and the master of the quarter mile, which is what drag racers go at it over.

We actually use her for flying records, which means terminal velocity. I hold one on her at 100 miles per hour – the fastest flying eighth of a mile at Elvington for a T100 Triumph. She is a monster. The engine's a 500cc Triumph, which is super-charged and runs on methanol. You lie on this grenade and it is totally and completely built for one thing only and that is to go as fast as you can on it.

Now, for me, if you're going to go quick – proper quick – do it on a track. I've pinned it on the road, in my youth, of course, and I've had the most wonderful times doing it, but you just can't any more. There are too many people, too many speed cameras and those days are over.

For something so brutal, it looks elegant, I think. It has what's called gorilla clamps on the head of the engine, so that it doesn't explode into your chest when you're lying on it.

The speed and acceleration you feel on it are fabulous. It is quicker than a race replica Fireblade. Fucking hell, man, you know you're alive riding that thing.

Obviously, it's utterly terrifying. You lie on it and it's burbling away and just making such a racket because its exhaust pipes are only two-foot long.

I'm always shitting myself. My massive fear is the chain coming off and wrapping round and locking up the rear wheel.

Then I launch it, and my ears go through my arsehole. The power is quite exceptional. You go through the gears and time stops because you're going so fast. You're in your own little bubble, and you hit the timing lights, then you wind her down, but you don't want the run to end.

It's bare-bones motorcycling, which life is all about, you know.

It's dangerous, but so what? My view is that you need – especially at my age – to consider what you're doing and why you're doing it on a motorcycle, but you've also got to live, man.

And fear is temporary; regret is permanent.

So you have to get over the fear – you have to conquer the fear, which makes you a better person all round.

If you live your life in fear, you won't achieve anything.

When you throw your leg over a bike like that, you do think, 'What the fuck am I doing?'

But I'll tell you what you're doing, son: you're living life and you're experiencing stuff other people are too chicken to experience.

Chapter 10

I did go back to school to do my exams.

I passed.

Only just, but who cares?

I didn't want to go to university.

I wanted to be a session drummer, man, and after leaving school, I spent a few hazy months attempting to follow that dream.

I session drummed at various little-known studios for dodgy bands around London and I definitely had an affinity with that scene.

Rock and roll, to me, is the ultimate in escapism – and rock and roll and motorcycles work so beautifully together because they're both about individualism. They're all about rebelling against the world and authority. They're about good times, you know? And when you marry a motorcycle with rock and roll, I think you get a very cool take on life.

The problem for me, when it came to rock and roll, was that I basically had no talent.

But that didn't stop me living the life.

I was in a band called Tannoy 7, and we actually supported Teardrop Explodes at the Lyceum. I really thought I was God. The problem is, I was so out of my head that I genuinely don't remember it. I was on another planet most of the time.

*

I guess eventually I realized I wasn't going to make it as a musician and moved back in with the parents, back down in Winchester.

Things had moved on there. As the bikes got bigger and more powerful, we started going up the M3 to London to get drugs. We used to draw lots on a Friday night as to who was going to go up.

Guy and I were exempt because we went once and never came back. We turned up in town and it was all happening, so we stayed and spent everyone's money.

Rob was the ringleader. He actually didn't ride bikes, he drove cars. His father had died and he was really rich, so he had a Lotus Esprit and a 911 Turbo and all this kind of stuff.

Anyway, thanks to Rob, we started getting into acid. (He's the most recent one to die – just a few years back, still looking for a needle.)

Now if you thought marijuana was bad, well, what a load of toxic crap acid is.

What could possibly possess you to drop a microdot, sit there, wait for it to come on and then, for eight hours, have no control over what's going to happen?

But I'd read about it, I'd played songs about it, I'd hung out at festivals and heard people who smelled telling me about it. I'd sat in tents listening to girls telling me about it, acting like I cared, when all I wanted was to get in their knickers.

So in the end, I took it.

And there I was, on a plateau where I couldn't ride a motorbike, or communicate, and seeing weird things coming out of the walls.

Why? *Why?*

I didn't want to be in a parallel universe. But I took it anyway, again and again.

We took amphetamine sulphate – speed. I mean, no wonder that stuff is three quid a gram with a free bag of wine gums thrown in. It makes you sweat, and it makes your cock the size of a button mushroom. That's basically it.

Oh, no, hang on . . . I forgot something! It also makes you unable to sleep for the whole night and most of the next day.

Anyway, the point is, Rob was going up to London a lot. He was a couple of years older than us, and he came down one day and said, 'Do you want to try some smack?'

And I said, 'What? Heroin?'

'Yeah,' he said. 'Do you want a line?'

'Can you snort it?'

'Yeah, I inject it because it's better, but you can snort it or smoke it, you know.'

So I had a line. It was like a line of coke, but brown. I snorted it. And then I waited. And then . . . for the first time in my life, I had this sense of completeness, of wellbeing. Then I was sick. And then I was sick again and then again – and then I had that feeling of wellbeing again.

Imagine you wake up in the morning in a lovely warm bed and you look at the clock. It says nine o'clock and you scream, 'I'm late for work!'

You jump out of bed, stressed out, freaking out – and then you realize it's Sunday.

You get back in bed and you lie down and you feel all cosy, warm, mellow and contented, with a sense of relief that you've escaped some awful appointment with doom.

That's heroin.

And that void that has eaten away at your insides for the last eighteen years?

Gone.

Disappeared.

But, even better, check this out: I could walk on it! I could think straight! I could behave completely normally!

We went out into town that evening, and I hailed a cab. It was such a small thing, but I remember being able to do that without feeling insecure. I was confident. Confident in a quiet, self-assured way.

And suddenly, even though I'd snorted just one line of it, I realized that out of all the shit, pathetic, sad drugs I'd been taking all my life – at long last, I'd found what I'd been looking for.

I spent probably a couple of months snorting away at the weekend, or on a Saturday or whatever, having a couple of little lines on the mirror: happy days.

But you progress very quickly from snorting it to smoking it.

Nobody starts taking heroin with the goal of becoming an addict, but it creeps up on you. You start by sniffing the odd line. But after a few weeks, that doesn't quite do it any more. So the next step is to chase the dragon. You get yourself a square of tin foil, six inches by six inches. You get another bit of tin foil that you roll around a pencil or a cigarette to make a tube, and you put ridges all the way down that tube. That's your smoker. Then you pour a small amount of heroin onto the foil. And I mean a really small amount. (A McDonald's coffee stirrer – you know those tiny spoons? – that's ten quid's worth, flattened off at the top. Half of that is a fiver's worth, and a fiver will last you, when you first start taking heroin, all weekend.) You put the powder on the foil, you put a lighter underneath the foil and the powder turns to brown liquid. You then tilt the foil and, obviously, the liquid runs down. As it runs you chase it, the ball of liquid, with your smoker – you chase 'the dragon' (the fumes coming off the ball) and you inhale. You hold it in with a quick toke of a cigarette, release – and your arsehole's gone through your ears, man.

It's fantastic. And there's still *loads* left on the foil. When you're first taking heroin, you probably have three chases, then you might go out to the pub or whatever, and then you'd have a couple more when you come home.

For the first six months, when you are just having it at the weekends, you're ranging between a five-, ten-, maybe a fifteen-quid bag, if you're really up for it.

And life is sweet.

Of course, there was one fundamental difference between being a public-school-posh-twat-addict like me and a street addict: I had money. I could borrow it, take it off my parents, earn it. But street junkies – they're waking up in the morning with nothing. So they've got to nick a fax machine before they get started.

I think that's why you never meet a stupid junkie. Junkies are the world's hustlers.

Anyway, at first, that ten-pound bag lasts all weekend. On Sunday night, you sit in bed and unravel the smoker. All the smoke you've sucked through it will have coagulated, so there's pure smack on there, which you can then resmoke through another smoker. It's a great way to end the weekend, gouching out with a snout on, watching the telly.

But then, a couple of weeks later, you might actually have it on Monday morning because you can't face Monday without it.

Then, your mate's coming down on Thursday, not Friday. So you have fifteen quid's worth.

Next, on Tuesday morning you think, Oh I've got a really bad cold.

But when your mate comes down on Wednesday night, you have a hoof and it's gone. You don't have a cold any more.

What? You thought that was a cold.

No. It was withdrawals. Cold turkey, or, as we called it, 'clucking'.

And because other people have got that feeling, you're all in it together, and you're becoming a sub-culture. It's all right to cluck a little bit, and to moan about clucking, and then the gear comes and everyone's happy.

And quite suddenly you're taking it every day. A small amount, but it's every day.

And addiction has crept up on you.

Chapter 11

Heroin didn't stop me getting a job. In fact, I think it gave me the confidence to decide what I wanted to do. I'd seen this picture – a Don McCullin shot, I think – of a dude in a Vietnam helicopter with a camera on his shoulder and a spliff on the go, and I just wanted to be that man.

So I told my mother – partly to placate my father – that I wanted to be a news cameraman.

Strangely enough, in Winchester, there was a production company that did camera crewing, and my mum went into their office and told them I'd work there for free.

'You did what, Mum?' I was incredulous.

The boss of that production company was a guy called Billy, and he rang me that night. His first words were, 'Did you go to Eton?'

'Yeah.'

'Well, come for an interview, then.'

So I went down to the interview and he said, 'I've never, ever seen an old Etonian. I just invited you down to see what you look like.'

He gave me a job as a runner. They paid me £150 a month. So my Eton education, bizarrely, opened that door for me.

I worked my way up to studio manager and I got on well with Billy. One of the first shows I ever worked on with him was a series called *Out of Town* with TV presenter Jack

Hargreaves. My responsibility was to look after Jack as a runner; the show made a huge impression on me and Jack quickly became one of my heroes.

For *Out of Town*, we simply went round to Jack's shed, set up our gear and he just sat there – no autocue or anything. He sat there in his shed and talked shit. And what incredible shit it was. I'd sit on set and listen to him, totally spellbound by his stories of the countryside and fishing and the old ways of country life. Then, after he told a story, he would talk about a prop – a weird piece of equipment he had with him – and he'd tell you what it was: maybe it was a fish hook; or, you know, a really odd thing like a pestle and mortar that was for crushing fish bones; or a special scythe that was actually for cutting linseed, not corn, and he'd tell you all about it. That would be part one; then, in part two, he'd go off and experience it. I think he was the inspiration for the guy in the shed coughing in *The Fast Show*, but Jack was a real pro, he'd never have been spluttering like that on camera.

Then there was Fred Dibnah. Fred Dibnah was an icon for me because, even back in the day when he was on TV, there was a good bit of bullshit about, but there was nothing fake about him, ever.

He had the greasy cloth cap, he had the legacy of his trade as a steeplejack, he had the constant fag hanging out of his mouth (he'd be on the vapes today) and he had a passion, an individuality and eccentricity that were brilliantly conveyed on TV.

Television was his perfect medium; I don't think people would have got him in print. To see him and see what he did so visually – it was ground-breaking television. His passion for British engineering – and for Britain – really stood out.

Those guys were legendary, and to this day I dream of being a Jack Hargreaves/Fred Dibnah crossover on wheels, riding around this great country on a classic British motorcycle, sharing my love and passion with an audience.

Anyway, it was all good, and I was happily working on *Out of Town* and doing a bit of news when one day, Billy came out of a meeting and said, 'I've had it with this production company. I'm out.'

'What do you mean, Billy? What are you doing?'

He said, 'I'm going to go to London to start a production company. Do you want to come with me?'

I was about nineteen and he was about thirty-six.

He said, 'I can't afford to pay you.'

I said, 'No change there, then.'

Then he said, 'Look, when we're filming I'll pay you fifty quid a day because I can afford to pay you then, but meantime I'll give you ten per cent of the business. What do you reckon?'

Why not? I thought. I had nothing to lose. And there were definitely going to be more women up in London than in Winchester.

So we set up this little production company, the two of us, called Straight Face Films. We were based in Archer Street, Soho, where all the jazz musicians hung out. The office was basically a broom cupboard that we blagged off a mate, but I didn't care.

I was in heaven. I was in Soho, man! I could carry film cans around town! I had my own production company (well, 10 per cent of it, but I didn't need to tell the birds that).

Amazingly, we actually started to get work for Channel 4. Our first show was about disabled people in Southampton writing newsletters. It went out at three o'clock on Channel 4 one Saturday afternoon, just as the FA Cup Final kicked off on the BBC. Literally nobody watched it. Rating: 0.0. Best thing I've ever seen on TV.

Then we started doing pop promos. Billy sat me down one day and he said, 'Mate, we're doing all right. I can pay you seventy-five quid a day.'

And I went, 'Well, can we have some company motorbikes?'

He said, 'Sure what do you want?'

'Well, I want a GSX-R1100.'

He said, 'Cool, mate.'

I said, 'Why don't you get one too? We'll get a deal on two.'

He goes, 'I don't want one because I've got a family, mate. I'm going to get a Volvo estate.'

'Fuck, all right.'

So he went and bought a new Volvo estate. I went and bought a GSX-R1100.

A week later, I'd just come off a video for this Irish flute player called James Galway when the phone rang.

It was Billy's wife.

Billy had been killed in his Volvo. He'd fallen asleep at the wheel. He'd gone off the road on the way back to Brighton, across the central reservation. The crash was head-on.

And I couldn't help thinking that if he'd just been on the GSX-R1100, he'd still be alive, because you don't fall asleep on a bike.

Russian Sidecar Outfit

I love these so much, I've got three.

Russian motorcycles and sidecar outfits came in different guises; they were called Dnepr, they were called Urals and they were called Nevals – but they were all marketed under the one name of Cossack, which the Russians thought was a great idea.

These, to me, are the coolest sidecar outfits in the world. You can pick one up for about three grand.

A sidecar is really an acquired taste, but for my money, it is definitely a design icon. Their history is that back in World War II, the Russians desperately needed any vehicle that was any good, and Stalin saw these BMW R72s being ridden by the Nazis and he thought, as you do, They're well coolski. They'll do the business. So what he did, through a Swedish spy, was he managed to acquire seven of the Nazis' BMW sidecar outfits, smuggled them over to Moscow and, basically, Russian engineers retro-engineered them to develop the Cossack outfit, which is *absolutely identical in every way* to the BMW. Everything. One of my outfits has a BMW speedo in it. All the parts are interchangeable, except the Russian one was made of monkey metal.

My favourite of the three is the 1968 Dnepr. That actual bike patrolled the Berlin Wall. It is totally original from 1968, and I bought it off the geezer who bought it back in 1970, working in East Germany.

Sammy and I have drunk tea in it (Sam's actually made tea in it) and we've also managed to swap from me being in the chair to being on the bike and from Sam riding it to being in the chair while we're going along.

People laugh, people point and people giggle at you, but it's good-natured. It's a public service to keep the nation happy. A smile a day keeps the pills away.

To me, you cannot have more fun for three grand than being in a Russian sidecar outfit. And also, just to top it off, it's got reverse gear for those difficult-to-get-into spaces. Try to do it fast and you get a massive tank slapper and nearly roll it.

Chapter 12

When Billy died, everything changed.

Of course, it was something that I was not prepared for. And when you're confronted in life with something that you're not prepared for, most people do one of three things: you run away (maybe not literally, just disappearing into a bottle or whatever); you allow your emotions to actually happen and you go through it, even if that means you are a complete emotional mess for two years; or you wheel out the stiff upper lip and carry on like nothing's changed.

I suppose it was inevitable that I'd end up favouring the stiff-upper-lip approach, combined with loads of drugs. I'd been brought up that way – to never show my emotions. It was an article of faith in my family. But I couldn't have got in touch with my emotions if I had wanted to: they had been completely suppressed because of the drugs I was taking.

For most addicts, the real value of drugs is to change the way you feel, either by masking or enhancing feelings. And that means you end up needing to take them all the time: all day, every day.

If you have a feeling of loneliness, you take drugs, it goes away; if you have a feeling of insecurity, you take drugs, it's gone; if you have a feeling that the world's caving in, you take drugs, and suddenly it seems it is all standing up just fine. And if you have a feeling that life is amazing, that this is fun – well, then drugs just make it a whole lot more of a blast.

Whatever the feelings are, there's a drug to enhance or suppress it. When Billy died, I was twenty-two, and I was extremely proficient at using and combining freebase cocaine and heroin to manage and contain every emotion to perfection.

On a practical level, of course, I didn't know what to do, so I just had to trust my gut. Billy's father-in-law, a butcher from Brighton, turned up one day and announced he was running the production company with me.

Sorry, mate? Maybe he thought that was the right thing for him to do, to protect his daughter. But, even at twenty-two, I knew it made no sense. So I told him I'd make sure Billy's widow got money and a company car, and he reluctantly agreed to bugger off.

It was a nightmare, that whole time. I sometimes felt like it was happening to somebody else. I was completely anaesthetized to it all because I was living in a permanent drug haze. The seductive power of heroin is that when you take it, you feel at peace, whatever is going on. But in the rare moments of sobriety, of clarity, the anguish and grief would just sweep over me, and suck me into a great despair.

I was incredibly close to Billy. At almost twenty years older than me, he was my father, really. He had guided me through my career – and suddenly he was gone. Gone and left me.

It was an anguish that only more gear could cure.

I think my life would have been very different if Billy hadn't died, because he would have sussed me out about my drug addiction. And I loved him so much I might actually have listened. Billy was the only person in my life who lovingly told me where I was going wrong.

No one I respected had the right combination of balls, inclination and knowledge to say: 'Henry, you're a dickhead, and you're a junkie.'

I had loads of junkies saying it to me though. One of the odd things about junkies is that we each think the guy shooting up next to us is worse than us, or a better prospect to be saved. So when someone with a needle hanging out their arm is saying, 'Henry, you need help,' it's pretty easy to think, Well, you're doing half a gram a day, man. And I don't inject, so I'm not really a junkie, am I?

But that couldn't be further from the truth. The only thing not injecting meant was that I avoided Aids, luckily.

So when Billy died, there was literally no one to give me any direction in life whatsoever.

Chapter 13

Straight Face Films was still based in the broom cupboard in Archer Street.

A news producer called Barry Fox rented us camera kit, and, after Billy died, I moved into a room in Soho above Barry's office. I mean, literally, a room and a bog.

Barry had about thirty crews out every day, going all over the world – Beirut, Israel, wherever – providing footage for the TV networks. Once in a while, a job would come in and they wouldn't have anyone available to cover it, and Barry, who knew I could operate a camera, would stick his head upstairs and say, 'Henry, can you go to Northern Ireland? Now? £350 a day?'

And I was just desperately trying to scratch a living, so I'd say, 'Sure thing, Baz,' and jump on the bike and go to the airport.

When I came back, he'd look at my footage and go, 'Wow! That's brilliant, Henry. How did you get so close?'

Well, it was brilliant because I was out of my head; standing there in the middle of a riot when everyone else was taking cover. Out of my fucking turret on smack.

It wasn't that I felt no fear – I remember being terrified; it was just that at the same time, I was very conscious of not giving a fuck, like I felt there was no point in living anyway. Consequently, I could get better shots than anyone else. And the praise I got made it easy for me to convince myself that I was succeeding, rather than putting myself emotionally, physically and spiritually in massive danger.

The stuff I saw doing news was unreal. It was hard to believe what was going on in Northern Ireland, while we were wrapped up in cotton wool just half an hour away, on this side of the Irish Sea. Religion as a system of control was so in your face. I remember this amazing feeling of futility there, the sense that this was never going to end.

I also went out to the Middle East. I went to Libya when the Americans bombed Tripoli. I covered riots, shootings, air crashes, sieges and Romanian revolutions. The smack kept me removed from it all emotionally, and as a news cameraman you have to nurture a certain detachment. But at the same time, you can't unsee that stuff. It seeps into your soul.

Much later, when I was clean, I went to Bosnia. Nothing could have prepared me for that. The death and horror I saw there were unbelievable.

I'm not a religious man, nor am I political. Maybe I was doing a service for humanity, filming all that shit, getting it on the news, but it didn't feel like it – because, as far as I was concerned, I was just doing it for the money, which actually meant the gear.

In Bosnia they called us lot *lješinar*, which means vulture. We pretended we didn't give a shit, but the truth is, that hit home. I did feel like a vulture, because I felt was preying on people's pain and anguish, sticking a camera in their faces for my own good and making money out of it.

And to me, even in my stoned state, that didn't sit well.

My Crazy Sidecar Sled

This outfit is a complete and total mongrel. I bought it off a guy called Chris down in Cornwall, and the motorcycle was a Z400, with a DTR125 front end, a BSA petrol tank and a CB350 Café Racer rear end. The sidecar is a Watsonian frame, a Steib sidecar body that Sam and I found in a hedge and a Morris Minor sidecar wheel.

This is what motorcycling is all about today. It's reminiscent of a post-World War II moment when it was all about making a bobber – taking a military bike, cutting it up and bobbing it – because you couldn't afford a new civilian bike.

Same thing happened in 2007, all the big choppers were bought on sub-prime loans, so when the credit crunch came, people took to building bikes in sheds again, cutting things up. Nothing was off-limits to customize. As long as you had an angle-grinder and a little bit of creativity, you could fill your boots, son.

That sidecar outfit, man, it flies. The front brake's a bit iffy, but generally, what a cool bike.

I defy anyone to hate that. It's great. My dog goes in it; my wife might even go in it, one day.

It may fall apart at any moment, but that adds to the fun.

Chapter 14

A lot of bombs were going off in London at that time, and the bike was handy to move film around fast. A bit too fast on occasion. I got nailed doing 98mph on The Mall on my 1100 Slabside on one occasion, and ended up in court.

Bow Street Magistrates' Court. And my lawyer comes running up all excited saying the cops have made a typo on the documents.

'They said that you were stopped by a police motorcyclist but actually you were stopped by a police Land Rover. So, if that's wrong, everything else must be!'

Oh, right, great.

So my lawyer stood up in court and went, 'Can I just draw, my Lord, your attention to this summons, which says Henry Cole was stopped by a police motorcycle? Actually, it was a *Land Rover* which eventually caught up with him at Sloane Square, after chasing him from Marble Arch?'

I'll never forget it, the magistrate just went, 'We're not here to discuss a typo.'

My lawyer was completely done over by that.

Then there was a break and my lawyer goes, 'Right, this is the scam. What we're going to do is we're going to tell them that this happened, and this happened. And blah blah blah, so that's the plan.'

There's this guy sitting next to us in plain clothes listening to everything we are saying.

And when the hearing starts up again, the judge says, 'Could we call the arresting officer?' And up steps the bloke sitting next to us.

So it's a fairly major legal disaster at this point, but my lawyer wasn't about to give up. About ten minutes later, he stood up and said, 'Mr Cole is a news cameraman, and if you take his licence off him and a bomb goes off, he's going to have to catch the bus.'

The judge sighed, 'Look, I happen to know one or two things about news coverage, and the sound man can drive the car, so can we move on?'

I was banned for a month and got a £580 fine. Result.

By this time, Guy had moved up to London and so we were living together, along with a bunch of other druggy bikers at a house in Elsynge Road in Wandsworth.

I was living a completely dual existence; by day, I was news crewing and also, as the business developed, starting to shoot corporate films for companies like ICI and IBM; but come the evening, I was just another junkie, going out, getting wasted whenever and wherever I possibly could.

And bikes were still my connection to the subculture.

There was a whole clan – maybe fifteen of us – in the house. Some people had bedrooms, but most of us just slept in sleeping bags on the living-room floor.

Once some dudes broke in. Climbed in through an upstairs window and came sneaking down the stairs, rather surprised to find a bunch of smackheads all lying on the floor, laughing their heads off.

We said, 'Mate, just open the door! Stick the kettle on while you're there, will you?'

I met my mate Paul when I was looking out of the window one morning and saw a guy getting on my bike. I thought he was trying to steal it. I went outside with all the lads, giving it, 'You're dead,' and all that, but he apologized, and so we invited him in for a cup of tea and a bong. He turned out to be a really nice guy, and we became mates.

It was all mad; a bike-fuelled remake of *Withnail and I*.

As I was quite often carrying quite a lot of drugs around on a daily basis, I started gravitating towards a motorcycle that didn't draw attention to me. When you've got 3 grams of smack on you, coming back from the dealer's, a GSX-R1100 with a full race pipe, tiny little number plate and a black visor is obviously going to attract some attention from *le filth*. So my bike of choice became an XJ650 Yamaha shaft-drive. It wasn't a shitter – it had a little bit of a nice loud can on it, but not too much, and an eight-inch-wide headlight. And it was anonymous.

That bike really flew. I'm sure other bikers will understand this, but I rode it much quicker than my GSX-R1100 round town, not because of the handling, but because I did not give a fuck. Let's say you're pinning it down the King's Road on that and you go for an overtake, but then you wonder, Oh, am I going to get in before that central island? Well, on the Gixer, you've got two and a half thousand quid's worth of faring that's going to hit the central bollard, so, you think twice. But on the XJ650? Fuck it, let's give it a whizz; I'll go round the outside if I don't get there in time.

This is what I don't get about people who go out with their bonus money and buy themselves a 30-grand Harley, a bagger with all the paniers. To actually go out and have a giggle, you know, it's best to have something you don't give a fuck about if you end up in a bush with it.

Sadly, my XJ650 bit the dust on Ebury Bridge Road. I had to hang a right on a mini roundabout one time and I just went down. I found myself on my arse sliding down Ebury Bridge Road, for no reason. There was no manhole cover there, no oil on the road, no diesel, it wasn't wet. I just went down. The only explanation I ever found was the camber was running away from me. Well, that and I was clucking, badly.

To this day, thirty-five years later, I am wary of right-hand mini roundabouts with the camber running away from me. I still go round them gingerly because of that accident. Skid then bought it off me and dropped a 750 engine into it. Guy dispatched on her for years after that.

I had another weird crash around that time: I was going down the King's Road one day on an XT250 motocross bike, a Yamaha (a motocross bike is handy for doing pavements in the city) and I saw this gorgeous girl come out of a restaurant called Blushes. I had quite a loud pipe on my XT250, so I dropped a cog and whacked it open, trying to get her to look at me.

And off I came.

I hit a central bollard outside Blushes.

I remember standing up and she had gone, didn't even know that I was trying to get her attention.

I was the only one in our crew who had a proper job; although Guy and his mate Simon had a gig pinstriping cars – literally putting pinstripes down the wings of cars. No one has them any more, but stripes were a big deal back then. Guy's stepfather had a company called Stylistic Auto, and they would print the stickers, then Guy and Si would get in their Golf GTi, and they'd go off and get wasted in some London car park, stripe 200 cars and make a mint.

The rest of the people we lived with were all riding dispatch round London. There was a big row of dispatch bikes outside the house, and every morning someone would have to get up and be the first person to turn the radios on. They weren't little devices like they have today; they were these great big megaphones on the backs of the bikes. And then whoever it was – we took turns – would come back in and they would also have to load the bong. Then everyone had a bong in their sleeping bags, and only then would we try and get to grips with life.

Now my life would collapse the minute I'd had the bong, and I would only really come round at about eleven o'clock, after I had got to work.

That's the life I led. And while it had its attractions, it also had its ramifications.

Everyone was dying around me the whole time. That's the main thing I remember. People were overdosing; people were hanging themselves. But the smack kept me at an emotional distance from it all. I'd hear about it, be sad for a bit, then smoke some smack and it all just disappeared.

Most weekends, I'd leave my drugged-up London family, get on the bike and go off to some public-school waster's house in the country.

I still got invited to quite a lot of posh parties. I remember going up on the GSX-R1100 to a wedding in Yorkshire one Saturday afternoon, massively late as usual, stoned out of my head, black tie on under the waterproof Rukka suit, toothbrush and a bit of money in my pocket. I met my mate Adam at Scotch Corner. He was a lunatic racer, a brilliant bike rider, and we pinned it up there.

As we came into the village there was the wedding party driving to the church. Me and Adam went past them at 120, literally pissed past this old Roller, both of us with full race exhaust pipes on our bikes.

The bride's father did not look happy with us when he made it to the church and saw our bikes racked up at the church. He'd have been even less happy if he knew I was smoking smack the moment I arrived and spent the whole ceremony totally gouching out.

Chapter 15

I basically became the posh crowd's official bit of rough.

I'd rock up at parties at houses in Chelsea with loads of smack and entice wannabe rebels without a cause into the bedroom and do smack with them. I was the king: I was in television, I had a big bike and loads of drugs.

It never occurred to me it was wrong to do that. And I genuinely don't think I understood that I was masking all those horrendous emotions about Billy's death and my own upbringing. I just thought these were the good times.

Every so often, the whole edifice would come crashing down and I'd have to move back in with the parents for a bit, commuting up and down from Winchester on the train while I got my shit together and found another flat in town.

I never saw my old man. I just sort of came home the odd night and went upstairs to bed.

Anyway, during one of these spells, I met this girl Tonya on the train, in the buffet car. She was a sweet, sweet girl, a secretary up in London, and, unluckily for her, she fell for me.

I managed to get a mortgage, Tonya's old man gave us the deposit and we bought a flat together – a studio flat in Brompton Park Crescent behind Fulham.

On the outside it looked like I was becoming a normal person, even a fairly successful one; I was in a relationship, going to work, travelling overseas to make films. But it was all a sham because I was still using. When I was making the shows, I was smuggling gear out of England in the cameras to keep me going.

Then Guy just completely disappeared. I lost contact with him. I didn't know where he'd gone. Just like all the rest of them, I thought.

Another problem was my new partner at Straight Face Films, Gary. Turns out, he was an alcoholic. So I was in the bog all the time taking smack (I'd rigged up the telephone with a super-long cord, so I could sit in the bog and indulge privately), while my partner had his secret cans of Special Brew in his desk. He was drinking his stuff, I was smoking mine – and we were both so obsessed with keeping our habits secret that neither of us realized what the other one was doing.

The company had no money; not because we weren't making any, but because I was smoking it all.

It was farcical.

I was always looking for easy ways to get off the smack for a bit. So when one day I got a call from Simon asking, 'Mate, do you want to come to the Monaco Grand Prix?' I said yes, because I thought it might be a good way of getting off the gear.

Simon had got in with some people from an auction house, who were renting a great big gaff in Monaco. He said, 'We can ride down there and stay for a week. We'll watch the practice on the Saturday and the race on the Sunday and then we'll ride back on the Monday. What do you reckon?'

Nice one, mate.

So I said to Tonya, 'Fancy coming on the back of the bike?'

And she said, 'Yeah. Ok.'

So, we got on the bike and we nailed it down there. But the moment I walked in I knew it was a disaster. There were all these *bloody nice blokes* – the types who work at the auction house and that kind of stuff, and it's basically a big PR stunt. They are just driving round in some flash vintage cars before they're auctioned.

I was given a room in the basement with Tonya.

I just so happened to have brought an eighth of an ounce of smack to help me taper off, and so I went down to the basement and I never came out. I never came out and felt the sunshine on my back . . . not once.

On the Saturday night – the night before the race – I ran out of gear.

I'd smoked it all. I had nothing left.

So I said to Tonya, 'Get dressed. We're going.'

'What? But the race is tomorrow.'

'But we've run out of gear, babe, and I've got a gram at home.'

'What do you mean?'

'We're going to ride back to London. Now. Ok?'

'But, Henry, it's midnight.'

'I know. Best get moving. Get the leathers on.'

It was pissing rain outside. But I didn't care.

I sparked the bike up in the middle of the village – full race pipe on – so that woke everyone up. And I pinned it in one go back to Calais – we stopped for fuel, but otherwise, one go. I didn't give a fuck that she was sitting on the back. Absolutely no consideration for her. I needed that smack.

I got back on the Sunday about lunchtime, got the gear and everything was ok for the next few hours.

But that trip was actually the catalyst for my whole life falling apart. Because I realized that I could not live a normal life. That my life was basically finished. That drugs, for whatever reason I got into them, were going to be the death of me.

In a way, before I met Tonya, the fact that I could not work out how to live my life wasn't a problem, because nothing mattered, no one else was getting hurt. I had a Golf GTi convertible, I had an XR3i convertible and I had one of those grey brick mobile phones that you had to carry around in a suitcase. I had everything. I didn't know how to run a business, so I never thought further than two months ahead. I'd go, 'I've got ten grand. Happy days. I'll get a load of gear.'

But then Tonya happened and I had to start thinking, 'Well, I may have just got ten grand but I've got bills of fifteen.'

And it pushed me over the edge.

About a month after that midnight run back from the South of France, Straight Face Films went bust. It was the Inland Revenue in the end who called it in.

So then I had to face facts: Billy's wife was going to lose the money I was paying her. Then Tonya left me. Just didn't come back to the flat one day. Poor girl.

I felt so guilty about her, not least because I dragged her down. All my fucking fault.

My life, my business – it was all destroyed, and I went into a really serious mental decline. I'd maintained that stiff upper lip until then: 'Tomorrow's going to be good; tomorrow everything is going to change.' But I quickly became suicidal.

Saxon Griffin Chopper

This is the wildest, most ludicrous motherfucker you're ever going to see. One crazy sled.

I needed a bike to go and do Route 66 revisited (my second ride on 66), and I'd seen and then bought a couple of bikes from this company called Saxon Motorcycles, based in Phoenix.

I'd bought a grey silver Prostreet from them – a sort of low-rider chopper – to do Highway 1 from San Francisco to LA and the American deserts, and I'd also bought a rat rod chop on which I did the east coast from Boston down to Key West.

So when I was pondering what to use for Route 66 revisited, the guys at Saxon said, 'Dude, we've got the top-of-the-range bike for you that we can trade for your other one.'

And I said, 'Ok, what's that?'

'It's a Saxon Griffin,' they told me.

'What the fuck is that?' I went.

And they said, 'It's just outrageous. It's got a 300mm rear tyre. Look,' Saxon said, 'we've got a blue one in stock, so we'll send it up to you. You can pick it up in Chicago.'

So we turned up at this place in Chicago to get my blue bike and there was *this* crazy chopper parked outside with the most incredible skulls paint job on it, right, in brown and yellow and flames.

I walked past it and I said to Hamish, 'That is one of the most ludicrous choppers I've ever seen in my life.'

I went into the guys and said, 'Hi guys. I've come to pick up the Griffin chopper – it's blue, I think.'

And the guy went, 'Dude, it ain't blue. It's the one outside.'

I went, 'What? It's that thing?'

And I rang Saxon and they said, 'We sold you the blue one, so we made you one with skulls and shit.'

So I'm heading out of Chicago on this thing, and it is virtually impossible to ride. I hit the back of the camera car a few times with the front wheel, coming up to traffic lights, because the front wheel was so far ahead of me, and I had to get used to it.

Anyway, I was wrangling with this thing at the start of Route 66 when I decided to have a word with it.

'Now, look, mate,' I said. 'So it's up to you. If you are nice to me and keep me safe all the way to Los Angeles, I will retire you to a warm carpeted garage in the UK where you don't have to do shit for the rest of your life. But if you fuck about, I'm going to make sure that I stitch you up with the next person who's going to radically rip you apart and customize you again.'

These are the kind of conversations I have with motorcycles.

Now, for me, the reason why I keep her is I don't break my word. If I say I'm going to do something, I'll do it. And that is really weird when you're talking about an inanimate object like a motorcycle, right? But at the same time, for me, spiritually, I said I'd retire her and that's it.

Saxons are part of history as well. They are the history of the credit crunch. All the American manufacturers who were making these crazy chops, like Saxon, like American Ironhorse, like Big Dog – they all got hit in the credit crunch because they were $45,000 bikes on fifteen-year finance with nothing down.

Hamish often says to me, 'Why don't you sell that?'

I go, 'Are you mad? I ain't selling that.'

Chapter 16

The thing that upset me the most was Guy. Where was he? Why hadn't he called me?

I kept thinking if Guy would just show up and we could smoke some gear, everything would be fine. But I had to find new people to use with. And that's how I ended up getting arrested by the anti-terrorist squad.

I was round at my dealer, Lloyd's, place in Fulham, about ten o'clock one morning. Usually, I'd go to Lloyd's on my slabby, but sometimes, when you're withdrawing really badly, you kind of need the safety of a car – that bubble, that layer of emotional insulation between you and the world. So I'd gone round in my brand-new Renault 5 GT Turbo (they were all the rage in the 80s). When I parked it up at the council-flat block and got out of the car, I noticed that there were a lot of workmen around. A bit odd, I thought, but I tried to tell myself it was just my junkie paranoia.

I rang the buzzer and prepared for a long wait, because I knew the buzzer went off in Lloyd's flat, but then he needed to walk down the corridor to press the button to speak and let me in.

Eventually, Lloyd's voice came through: 'Hello?'

'It's Henry.'

'Cool, man, come on up.'

I went up and into the flat. He took one look at me and said, 'You need to get well.'

So he brought out a quarter of an ounce of smack, threw it down, and said, 'Help yourself. I'll make you tea.'

I was chasing the dragon when the buzzer went again. Off Lloyd went on the long walk.

But he just didn't come back. He was in his dressing gown, and after five minutes, I was seriously wondering where the hell he had gone.

And then I suddenly started thinking about all the workmen outside, and just as it dawned on me that I had maybe walked into some kind of situation, a hammering started on the door.

'Number six, come to the door now!'

Was I in number six? Yes, I was in number six. So this was obviously a bust.

I rolled the smack up and threw it under the sofa, then got up and walked towards the door. Lloyd had actually left it ajar because, outside, I could just make out this massive police dog.

'Put your hands up. Put your hands out through the door first.'

I put my hands out. I had a cigarette on the go and a voice yelled, 'Drop the fag, drop the fag.'

Ok, man.

'Take one pace out into the corridor with your hands in the air.'

So out I stepped. I looked to my left down the corridor and there were these three geezers in blue boiler suits and blue berets, and they had got 303 rifles pointed at me.

I turned to my right and there was a guy with a pistol.

'Are you armed?' one shouted.

'I'm not armed. Jesus Christ what are you doing?' I said.

The geezer with the pistol said, 'Walk towards me, walk towards me.'

And I went, 'Right-oh.'

And then another geezer on my other side went, 'Walk towards me, walk towards me.'

I went, 'For Christ's sake, lads, I'm not armed, I'm not moving, you've just got to come and get me, all right?'

Another geezer in a blue beret without a gun came out from behind one of the shields, threw me against the wall and dragged me by the hair to the far end of the corridor where I was reunited with Lloyd, still in his dressing gown, looking like a rabbit in headlights.

They got me behind the shields and this geezer pushed me up against the wall, saying, 'Hello, Henry. Jones, Flying Squad.'

I said, 'What are you doing?'

He said, 'You smoke, don't you? Do you want a fag?'

I said, 'I can't smoke, they told me to drop the fag.'

And he went, 'Here, have one.'

And he stuck this red Marlboro in my gob and lit it.

'So, er, what is going on?'

He said, 'I'll tell you in a minute.'

And with that, I looked round and they're all going, 'Clear, clear, clear.'

And all the radios are going, 'Suspects apprehended.'

Anyway, to cut a long story short we were dragged back into the flat, and this guy, Jones, he said, 'Sorry about that, Henry. I had a hunch we got the wrong bloke when we started the operation. But it took a little bit of time for the car check to come through. The guy we are looking for fitted your description perfectly, except he was driving a white Datsun Cherry, rotted to fuck. He left his dog at Lloyd's here last night—'

Just then, this dog I knew nothing about appeared.

'And then he went round Southall and shot two dealers. And we thought you were him coming back for his pooch ...'

It was a crazy day, which only got crazier when the Fulham drug squad turned up.

'Hey, Lloyd, how you doing?' they said. They started taking the piss out of his accent, and then they said, 'Look, we're not going to bust you today, man, so just put the tea on.'

So we had a little cup of tea, me, Lloyd and the Fulham drug squad, while PT17 or whatever were all putting their shooters away.

Then, one of them asked me to open my briefcase, and they found, literally, ten quid's worth of gear.

And they go, 'Sorry, Henry, man, we've got to bust you. The boss with the braid on is here.'

I couldn't believe it!

One of the cops said, 'We'll have to go down to Fulham police station, mate, sorry. Can I drive your new Renault 5 Turbo? You can come in the back if you want.'

'Yeah, all right,' I said.

So we went down to Fulham police station and they interrogated me, and, to cut another long story short, they eventually said, 'Right, we're just going to give you a caution.'

And they went up to the desk sergeant and said, 'We're cautioning Mr Cole for the drug-squad guys.'

The desk sergeant looked up and said, 'You can't caution for class A narcotics. You've got to arrest him, for being in possession.'

And I'll never forget, the guy leaned over to the desk sergeant and said, 'Look mate, I can do what the fuck I want, now fuck off.'

And with that I was offski.

That was the last of my interactions with the police until after I got clean a few months later, and all my bikes were stolen.

My GSXRs were nicked and I got a phone call from the head of the vehicle-robbery squad at Chalk Farm police, Ken Jermyn, when they found them. Ken, who became a mate, rang up, saying: 'Henry, do you want the good news or the bad?'

I asked, 'What's the bad news?'

He said, 'We followed the ringleader of the bike gang up to Snetterton, and he was racing on your bike, and when he finished the race we put a roadblock up and we lost him. That's the bad news.'

I said, 'What's the good news?'

'He came fourth on your bike in the final race.'

Ken was cool, and they invited me to the car-robbery squad Christmas party.

I went along. One of the many joys of recovery. And the shooters in Fulham – the PT17 – they were there as well.

'Do we know you?'

I said, 'I think you might.'

And they went, 'Derek, come over. This is the guy in the cashmere.'

I said, 'What are you talking about?'

He explained, 'I remember that bust in Fulham at the council estate. I tell you what, we all laughed our heads off when we finished. None of us had ever pointed guns at a guy in a cashmere jersey and corduroy trousers before!'

Chapter 17

Still no sign of Guy.

I didn't even hear from him after our mate Matt Lambert died. I started thinking he must be dead too, which triggered another half-hearted attempt to get clean.

A successful musician I'd met doing a pop promo back in the day invited me down to his place in Wiltshire to dry out. So I got on the bike – still a Gixer, my staple ride for the decade – and I went down to the country for a week.

And I gave up the gear.

Didn't take any for a whole week.

But I did take coke, speed, acid and a lot of weed. And I drank a lot.

So I knew it was bullshit, really. And at about three in the morning on the Saturday morning, I thought, Sod this, I'm leaving. I'm going back to London.

So I drove back up at three, four in the morning – summer, really warm, getting light – and all I could think about was getting some gear.

I was riding back up the M4, and around junction 12, I started crying in my helmet.

Everything was broken. Everything was ruined. I was screwed.

My whole life had collapsed.

I was broke.

I was a heroin addict.

I'd let everyone down.

I felt utterly worthless; a piece of shit.

I said to myself, 'I ain't ever going to get off this heroin shit. I'm going to kill myself. I'm going to do it now.'

There was one car ahead of me on the motorway.

A Rover. Green, I remember.

I was near Cheveley, near Reading services. I lifted up my legs behind me, lay down on the bike, shut my eyes, dropped a cog, opened her up and aimed for the car.

I'm going to hit that car, I thought. I reckon I can get up to 140, 145 and hit it up the arse and that's got to kill me.

So I was lying on the bike, face down, pinned to the seat and after a while I thought, I should have hit it by now.

I sat up and looked in my mirror. I'd missed the fucker.

I pulled into the hard shoulder and smoked a lot of fags. I started to cry again.

I can't even kill myself, I'm that shit, I thought.

Then I rang my dealer.

A few weeks later, I tried to kill myself again, on High Street Kensington, driving into a shop front.

I had stopped paying the mortgage on the flat when Tonya moved out, and not long after the suicide attempts the repo' men started arriving.

Nice guys, mostly. Just doing a job.

Which happened to involve taking all my stuff.

Nothing personal.

I could respect that.

Bit by bit, they took everything. They took my Renault 5 Turbo, then my XR3i convertible, then the telly, then the bikes and then the flat itself.

I was left with one slabby that I had bought back off the insurance for six hundred quid. So I was left with a blue sausage bag of clothes strapped to my Gixer and a fifty-grand overdraft.

But in a way losing all the stuff was a relief.

I wanted to be that rebel which motorcycling embodied. I wanted to be a person, not an androgynous twat in a flat with a bird and a soft-top car.

I wanted life on my terms. As an individual. And motorcycling – the thing I had tried to kill myself with – was one of the things that made me want to carry on. Going out on the bike was my salvation.

Which brings me to the A3 somewhere near Oxshott, the Alsatian in the middle of the road (I can still see his face) and the world standing still.

There are three distinct phases to a motorcycle accident.

One: you realize you've lost control of the bike. Check.

Two: you prepare yourself, however briefly, for what's going to happen when you hit the ground. Check.

Three: the biggie; you hit the ground.

BANG.

So let's talk about crashing. You know, sliding down the tarmac, eating asphalt, dislocating your shoulders, breaking your arms, smashing your legs.

Let's discuss the ever-present possibility of death.

Motorcycling, my friends, is not safe. If you ride a bike for any length of time, you will come off. In fact, you can't really progress without coming off. And as long as you come up smiling, every crash makes you a better rider.

Sometimes, of course, you don't. It's a bit like getting clean. Some people get to rehab before they've overdosed and killed themselves, and emerge wiser for the experience; but, you know, some don't.

Every biker has a parent, a wife, a kid, a friend or a nervous business partner who objects to them riding motorbikes on the grounds that it's unsafe.

And they are right to worry. Statistically, motorcycling is absurdly dangerous. One per cent of the traffic in London is comprised of motorbikes, but they account for 22 per cent of the fatalities in that fine town (which is very unfair when you consider that most car owners in London drive like complete and utter pillocks).

But all those kindly, concerned friends and family members just don't understand. You don't ride a motorbike because you want to be safe. The closer you are to doing something nasty to yourself, the more alive you feel.

So what actually causes crashes?

Three things, basically: a) Inexperience. b) Speed. c) Other cunts.

This is why the most dangerous time to be a biker is just after you think you've sussed it: you've got your clutch control sorted; you've driven really quick down the road; you've gone into a bend and got it right; you know the bike and you've passed the test. And that's the exact moment when you are in the most danger.

Why?

Well, if you're a multimillionaire, you go out and buy a Lamborghini, and, happy days, you can go at 20 miles per hour down the King's Road and give it large. But on a motorbike you can't just sit there and keep up with the traffic, tootling along. You have to be *good* at riding.

But when you're new, you are innately inexperienced, even if you think you know it all.

For example, when I go into a corner, I'm always prepared (now) for gravel, and I'm always prepared (now) for oil, and I'm always prepared (now) for manhole covers. Going down a line of traffic in London, I will stop the minute I see an opening – a gap between two cars which are nose to tail – because I know if there's a gap in the traffic, some twat's coming out.

When I was a kid (and I'm talking up to the age of twenty-five here), I'd think, Let's just keep going, and I T-boned some poor sod badly on High Street Kensington doing exactly that: someone was pulling a U-turn and I went straight into them.

So that's inexperience.

And speed, well, when you are absolutely caning it, of course, you're more likely to do something nasty, especially if you are inexperienced at dealing with the motorbike at speed.

But other road users are the biggest danger by far.

Experience counts here as well. For example, if there's a car with a couple of dents in it ahead, I stay well away because if they haven't got the dents fixed, they probably don't give a shit about them. Their car is merely a device with which to hit a motorcycle.

And there are other things to watch out for that you learn over time.

Are they driving a Volvo estate?

Do they have a Belgian number plate?

If the answer to either of these questions is yes, then stay several miles away from them because they are likely one chromosome short of a potato.

New Hudson Autocycle

This is one of those classic vehicles that have been almost totally forgotten today, but changed the shape of society in their own era. In the 50s, these Autocycles were everywhere. Conceived as a crossover between a push bike and a motorbike, the New Hudson was the quintessential commuter bike.

Anyone – any working man or woman – could afford one. They would get on that and fuffle along to their job at the factory or whatever, and it was an incredibly cheap form of motorized transport that revolutionized millions of people's lives.

It wouldn't have looked like it does today back then – it would have had a fairing and knee guards on it – all that kind of stuff. But a lot of it was gone when I found that bike in a shed.

The bloke whose shed it was went, 'I reckon you're going to like this, Henry.'

I said, 'I do. How much do you want for it?'

'Nine hundred quid.'

I went, 'All right.'

So Alan Milliard turned up, he stripped the engine within half an hour, rebuilt it, relocated all the throttle cables – advance and retard, everything. I got on it, and it flew. I ride it a surprising amount, actually – at least two or three times a week. I found the VIN and recovered the V5 registration number for it. So it's fully legal, which I am really proud of.

Getting your hands on a bike like this and bringing it back to life is just such a kick. I feel the excitement of the guy who owned it in 1953, and I wonder about him and his life sometimes.

Chapter 18

U nlike us motorcyclists, car drivers haven't really got with the programme in the sense of understanding that the more expensive your car is, the more people hate you. Yet they believe it about other people, by which I mean they may be driving along and ask, 'Who's that twat in the Range Rover?' then in the same breath say to their passenger, 'Now, what about the BMW X5 that we're after?'

I really don't understand the car driver's mentality. For example, if you can't afford a Porsche 911, why would you decide to get a Porsche Boxster? What you're actually saying, as you drive along, is: 'I don't have enough money to deliver the image that I want to portray, so in the meantime I'll be a chippy fuck in a cheap Porsche.' It's all about what's happening next door, and how they want to be perceived by the neighbours, rather than having a utilitarian vehicle to get from A to B.

If you're driving the latest 911, fully blinged up, well, big respect to you, yeah. But if you're aspiring to do that and can't afford it, wouldn't it be better to restore an old classic something? Do something that's cool, rather than getting a Porsche Boxster for six hundred quid a month on the never-never?

If you drive a Golf, or a Skoda or a Land Rover, you could be a duke or a dustman. Isn't that the best way to be perceived? There's no hope for people who drive a Porsche

Boxster, especially in red. You know, why would you do that?

An Audi driver to me personifies modern mediocrity. He normally has oblong, reactalite glasses, a Hugo Boss suit and he is really impressed with his LED indicators, which, as far as I can tell, are the only things that differentiates the Audi models. They stream from left to right on the posher models. Wooppee doo.

And let's be honest, it takes a very special kind of wanker to drive a Roller; someone who literally does not give a fuck about how they're seen. Not only are new Rolls-Royce drivers hated, they are often verbally abused in traffic.

And then we have the Aston Martin.

Listen, mate, I get it. James Bond was cool. But he could do shit.

You've made enough money and you've got some style, so go ahead and get one. But I suspect you are more James Blunt than James Bond. The idea of you actually getting out of the motor and running after someone who has nicked the wife's handbag is questionable.

And if you are going to buy a cool car, don't leave it too late. I was once with Malcolm McDowell, the actor – a man who has great taste and a great take on life – when he looked at his E-Type, then looked at me and said, 'Why the fuck didn't I have one of these when I was twenty-one? Then people would have thought I was cool. Now they just think I'm an old cunt in a lovely motor.' (For some reason, old geezers on beautiful motorcycles still look – and feel – cool.)

Possibly the unluckiest car ever is the Lexus. On paper, it is the most fantastic car: it has every electronic gizmo you could possibly want; it's fuel efficient, dual fuel, comfortable, fast. It has all the latest gadgetry, everything. But would you have it on your drive?

No. I mean, I'd actually rather have a trike.

(A brief aside: why do people ride trikes? Well, I used to laugh at them, but they have certain plus points: you can ride one without a crash helmet; you can put dogs on them; you can put the family on them; you can take a load more luggage on a trike; you can eat an ice cream on one; you could probably make phone calls on one; and you can definitely listen to exceptionally loud music on a trike. You can, on the right one, look cool, in a FTW kind of way, as long as they haven't got a Volkswagen engine.

There are people who are making and designing unbelievably cool trikes. Harley actually manufacture a production trike. Now, I wouldn't own one myself, but at the same time I can understand why people do. I'm right up for vehicles that imbue you with a righteous sense of your own individuality and personality. And if you think you look the fucking doll on a trike, then, fill your boots.)

Chapter 19

You've got to be able to ride good to look good, which means that you've got to be emotionally attached to motorcycling as an endeavour.

When motorcycling, you can be really cool for about two grand and you also can't buy it.

It doesn't matter what bike you've got, or how much you spent on it: if you can't ride it, you can't ride it.

The born-again biker is probably in the most trouble of all. This guy giving it large at Goldman Sachs gets his nice little bonus. He already has his tasty house in Fulham and his XC90, but he wants to be a rebel at the weekends, so he goes and buys himself a bike.

He won't buy himself a 300cc, a 350cc or even a 500cc bike though.

No.

He'll buy himself a Yamaha R1 which will do 0–60 in 2.6 seconds – just because he can. To show off to his mates. But the fact is, he hasn't the faintest idea how to ride that machine. Everything happens so quickly on a bike like that, and this guy hasn't got the experience to react that fast.

This is not to say that just because you are fifty you can't start motorcycling, or take it up again if, say, you had a 50cc when you were a kid.

You absolutely can, but if you don't approach it with humility, you're toast.

Just buy yourself a 125 or a 250 – something you can grow with as a rider. Accept that you know absolutely nothing, and you'll be no more likely to kill yourself than anyone else. It doesn't matter how old you are, you're never too old to learn. It just might take a little bit longer.

So put aside your bonus and your economic clout and go and buy a Suzuki Hayabusa. If you really want to buy the Harley, fine. Go out, spend your thirty grand – but just have a fag and look at it in the garage while you learn again. Because you've got to get back to basics. You might think, at the age of fifty, How could I ever be seen on a little 125 motorbike? But that's what you've got to do, man.

You need to ride a motorcycle that you're not scared of. Even if you rode around like a lunatic in the 80s, you still need to go back to basics because everything has changed since then – the roads, motorcycles and, most especially, your reaction times.

If you're new, be aware that the most dangerous time to ride a motorcycle is when the weather has been dry for a long period and then it suddenly rains.

Rain is something to respect and something to embrace and something to love as a motorcyclist, weirdly. But if it rains after a long period of dryness, all the oil, bitumen, rubber and detritus on the road that usually get washed off by the rain have accumulated, so there is way more of it on the road than usual. Then, when the water finally comes, it mixes with all that shit, and I'm no scientist, but I tell you what – it's like an ice rink.

The most vivid example I ever had of this was crossing the Nullarbor Plain in Australia where it hadn't rained for several years, and suddenly there was a downpour.

Life became quite interesting, know what I mean? The whole road was covered with this kind of strange liquid, like an oil slick, and incredibly slippy.

Again, you know, riding a motorcycle in the rain is an incredible leveller. You suddenly realize that you could run out of talent very quickly. And the talent is basically to chill out, go slower and use an equal amount of brake front and back.

Of course you can just wait for it to stop, but to me, riding in the rain is like life.

If you think you know how to ride a bike, but you're scared of riding in the rain, you don't know how to ride a bike. The stuff that you learn in rain is amazing: when the front wheel slides, when the rear wheel slides, when it slides in braking, when you overcook the front brake, et cetera. You learn so much. For instance, when you're going over a zebra crossing, only go over the black bits, don't go over the white bits, right? Avoid like fuck any white bits of paint on the road, otherwise you're going to come off.

Then you take that knowledge back with you into normal conditions. For example, it is through riding in the wet that you learn not to panic when the back wheel snakes.

For instance, coming in on the A3 into London, there is a ton of this black tarmac – the black tar that they fill the cracks with. And it's slippy as hell. If you ain't ever ridden in the wet, you could well come off there; but if you have, you know what to do: keep your front wheel straight and let the back snake around, and don't freak out, because you know that it ain't going to be enough to take you off unless you panic and brake heavily. Then you are down like a sack of shit.

You also learn a lot about yourself when you're wet, cold, concentrating and when your life depends on every decision you make, which is absolutely true when you're riding in rain.

There's only one time that I've actually gone, Fuck this, I'm getting off. I'm not riding another wheel further. I was on my way to interview Gloria Estefan when I was caught in a tropical storm in Florida. The cars in front of me were sliding off the road on the freeway, skidding like skittles because they were aquaplaning. I was on this massive chop, and I saw an exit slip and I rode up the exit slip and pulled up. Hamish and Steve were behind me in the camera car, and I went, 'Gloria Estefan can fuck off!'.

I didn't like her music anyway, so we didn't interview her.

Whether you've got talent or not, if you're aquaplaning, get out. You can't carry on.

So rain, yes, definitely, get out there. But snow and ice? No.

I've been riding in snow, and it doesn't matter how talented you are – if you go into a corner and there's ice on it, you're in the hedge.

I've ridden through settling hail and snow in Norway. You can pick your way through it, but it's unpleasant, and you can easily kill yourself, so why bother? That's when cars come in handy.

Another bit of advice I wish I could tell these kiddies is, when you're pinning it on a bike, make sure that you're not overtaking when there are junction roads coming onto your road, even if they are on the other side.

I'm obsessed by safety. Saying this, I'll probably get run over tomorrow, but I've been riding bikes for forty-plus years without a break, and I haven't so far been killed.

Here's my philosophy.

Do everything really slow.

If someone who you're riding with is being a cunt, let them go. People trying to race you off the lights? Fuck 'em. Best of luck, mate. Anyone can ride a bike quick, but I bet they can't stop it in a corner when they need to.

Slow into the corner, fast out.

Every time you're turning right or left, look over your shoulder. *Don't just use your mirror.*

A friend of mine on a bicycle was nearly killed the other day because he used the little mirror on his bicycle, turned right and a guy was right up his arse, trying to overtake him. And the guy mangled him.

Wear the right gear. Wear an airbag. I do. They're incredible; little waistcoats that are attached to the bike. If I fall off, I blow up like the Michelin man. When I'm racing, I'll wear full leathers, back protector, neck brace, the whole nine yards. For the road motorcycling I do, I wear Kevlar jeans and half-boots that look like DMs and a leather jacket with and an open face lid.

I don't wear the heated jackets though. I'd rather drive a Reliant Robin that plug my wires into my motorcycle, if you know what I mean.

Guy is covered in wires. I was on a ride with him the other day. He gets on his BMW RR and I kick my Norton and it's going and I'm ready to fucking go and I'm waiting for him to plug into his fucking life. He's got wires coming out of his bollocks, he's got wires for his trousers, he's got wires coming out of his jacket, he's even got wires coming out of his gloves, you know. By the time he's got caught up with it, we could have been there. We could have arrived where we're going.

Brough Superior 1150

Uncle Dick Redbeard had one of these in the corner of his shed. So can you imagine how I felt when Mark Upham, the boss of Brough Superior, rang me and, in his inimitable way he went, 'My dear boy, now then. I hope you've got your cheque book out.'

And I said, 'What cheque book?'

And he went, 'Well, you must be in a position to acquire a Brough.'

I said, 'Well, I'm not really, Mark.'

'Well, you need to be. I've got one here which is an 1150 tourer from 1937 and it's matching numbers, so it hasn't been tampered with at all. It's in oily-rag condition, a rider's bike, and I want you to own it.'

I said, 'Mate, I want to own it as well, you've sold it. But how do I buy it?'

He goes, 'What have you got to swap?'

To cut a long story short, after placating the wife with a couple of nights away and the guarantee of a new kitchen in a few years and that kind of stuff, I swapped nine motorcycles and twenty-five grand for it.

This bike had been exported to New Zealand in 1937 and then it was repatriated in the 50s.

It was mechanically perfect.

The reason why Brough Superiors were ridiculously expensive when they were made was because the build quality and performance were quite exceptional. George Brough only ever used the very best components available to him (which was the aspiration that we had for Gladstone), and he created the frame and tank and everything in his style.

When you ride that motorcycle, it is just quite incredible to think that it still handles so well today. It has fabulous torque. I can cruise at 70, no problem. I can pull away in third. That's just how it handles, how the engine performs, eighty years later.

It is a gentleman's relish bike. Every time I ride it, I want to grow a handlebar moustache.

You turn up somewhere and everyone's around it for the right reasons, which is not about you, but about the motorcycle.

Three thousand Brough Superiors were built all told, of which around 1800 are known to be in existence. So 1200 are unaccounted for, and that's why the holy grail for me is to find one in a shed.

The Brough is the pinnacle of my life. After my wife, my kids and my dog, it's owning a Brough Superior.

What a privilege to curate such a jewel of British engineering.

Chapter 20

I see these kiddies going twice the speed limit through my village in Oxfordshire. If you reckon that's cool, then go for it, but the bottom line is that one day, with that level of inexperience – because you must be inexperienced if you're tear-arseing that quickly through a village – a tractor's going to come out and you're Elvis.

Be honest about it. If you ride a motorcycle on a regular basis, you've got a much bigger chance of killing yourself than if you're in a car.

As mentioned previously, a rookie rider in London statistically is in great danger.

But if you actually sit down and contemplate your life as a biker, that's part of it. It's part of rejecting this bubble-gum society, this nanny state. It's the price we pay for freedom, individualism and a contentment that is very difficult to attain moving around in one of those fucking tin boxes everyone wants us to use.

Still, safety-wise, we've all got to wake up and smell the coffee and understand that if we want to be Valentino Rossi, where does Valentino Rossi do it?

On.

A.

Track.

I love speed.

But for me, if you're going to go quick, proper quick, just do it on a track, mate.

I've done it on the road – in my youth, of course – and I've had the most wonderful times doing it, but, you just can't do it any more. There are too many people, too many speed cameras and those days are over for me.

It's probably partly down to having kids.

My wife, Janie, and I really wanted kids but it was difficult for us. Janie would get pregnant, but wouldn't be able to hold on to the pregnancy. For reasons that medical science hasn't ever established, we went through a horrendous few years in which we had five miscarriages. All the specialists told us: there is nothing wrong, we don't know what it is, so just carry on, keep trying.

In one way, that was great news, but in another way it was like, 'Oh, my God, do we emotionally have to go through all this again?'

So it was a two- or three-year period of desperation. We couldn't really accept that we weren't going to have children. We bought a dog, like everybody else, and loved it to death, and, to cut a long story short, Janie did get pregnant and did go to full term. And then Charlie appeared, which was amazing.

Charlie's got eight godparents, because we thought, Well we're never going to have another. And then, with the pressure off, Tom came along!

I must say, when the ankle biters arrive, that's a huge moment for any relationship.

I'm really glad in a way that we had kids so late in life. I mean it's a bit embarrassing in the school car park these days, because I'm like twenty years older than any of the other parents, but the advantage is we genuinely did not want to stay out all night and party and then have a 5am feed to deal with. Janie and I had a ball together, pre-children, but I was definitely very immature. I think I needed those extra twenty years.

The best advice I was ever given about children was from a mate who told me, 'You'll be amazed how little money, but how much love and tolerance you need for your child at first, and then later on, as they get older, you'll be amazed how much money *and* how much love and tolerance they will need.'

But I do think it is actually what life is all about – and not just because one day Charlie and Tom might look after me, when I'm on my drip, you know, in my wheelchair. It's about leaving a little legacy. Maybe that's arrogant, but I don't think so. I'm never going to be Zeffirelli, I'm never going to be Graham Norton but, you know, Tom or Charlie might, and they'll be sitting there in an interview one day going, 'Yeah, my dad, he was a bit of a weirdo, and he presented these weird shows about motorbikes. He gave me the inspiration to get where I am.'

Having kids was an incredible rollercoaster of emotions, because we never, ever thought we'd even have one, so to have two is a miracle.

It also does change how you ride a bike. Parenthood coincided with me not going quick on the roads. Going quick on a track, at least I know there's an ambulance at the end of the run if it all goes wrong.

The trouble is, it's terribly dangerous if you get on a motorcycle thinking, I've got to be careful here and not do this and not do that because I've got kids now.

Every time I leave the door on a *World's Greatest Motorcycle Ride*, a part of me thinks I won't see them again, and that's something I try to get out of my head by the time I get to the airport.

But I have to admit I haven't exactly pushed motorcycling to my kids.

They are surrounded by bikes and it's up to them whether they come out to the sheds or not. Tom's got an XR70 motocrosser, but he's also a really good footballer. I sometimes think he might have a career in sport, in athletics, so him motocrossing and breaking his ankle might not be the best result.

But if your kids do want to have a go, then off-road is the way to go. As a parent, you want to keep them off the road as long as possible. Off-road, you throw yourself against the countryside, and, generally, the worst that's going to happen (and yes there are tragic exceptions, obviously) is that they'll break a leg or an arm.

If you get T-boned by a car at fourteen riding illegally, you're probably dead. But off-roading, you crash because you've run out of talent, rather than some other wanker nailing you, so it is the best place to learn. In a nutshell, if your kid has a passion for motorcycling, then get him or her the right tuition in the right environment.

Don't turn a blind eye. Don't think, I'm not going to get involved in this. Because then they will go off and ride illegally.

Try to embrace the relationship and their passion and, hopefully, once they've come off a couple of times moto-crossing, they'll understand how to ride safely at a very deep level when it comes to riding on the roads.

Chapter 21

Motorbike riders do tend to see the inside of hospitals more than other road users.

My most recent trip to the hospital was after I broke my shoulder in three places motocrossing.

I came off, and I could feel that my shoulder was not where it should have been. I got to Hemel Hempstead A&E and they went, 'Look, have a couple of paracetamols. A doctor will be with you.' And then I showed the woman my shoulder and she went, 'Actually, on second thoughts, I'm going to get an ambulance for you to go to Watford now.'

I got in the ambulance and the geezer went, 'Right, I'm going to give you some morphine.'

I said, 'Look, I'm an old heroin addict. I don't want any of my drug of choice, thanks.'

So he said, 'Well then, the only thing I can offer you for the pain is this gas-and-air stuff.'

I went, 'What's that shit?'

He said, 'Well, have a breathe on that; get on that cylinder.'

So the old blues and twos were wailing and I was going to Watford because the shoulder was officially well fucked, and I was having a go on the gas and air.

I got to Watford and they wheeled me in. And as they were getting me out of the ambulance, I said, 'Oh, I think that cylinder's empty.'

He went, 'What? No one's ever emptied that cylinder.'

I went, 'Well, I think I might just have done that.'

Everyone always seems to be slagging the NHS. All I know is when you come off a motorcycle, they could not be more professional.

They were amazing. They always have been, with all my misdemeanours.

I'm sure when you're lying there unconscious, they're going, 'Fucking idiot bikers, when are they ever going to learn?' But they never convey that to you.

And weirdly, when you're lying in a hospital bed after coming off, do you think to yourself, I shouldn't be riding a bike?

No.

That's the stupid addiction of motorcycling.

You don't want to capitulate, put your hands up and go, 'All right. I'll get a Nissan Micra.'

I might regret that I've run out of talent or that someone's pulled out on me, but do I regret that I was on a motorbike? Perhaps if I was crippled for life I would, yes. But if I walk away, then I still love the motorcycle; I still understand why I ride it.

Conor Cummins is a TT rider and one of my heroes. He came off on a section of the Isle of Man TT circuit called the Verandah. He had a front-wheel blowout. It wasn't his fault. But he came off at 150 and went over the cliff.

I went round to see him at his house in the Isle of Man about three weeks after the accident. Both legs were in cages.

I sat there. 'Conor, mate,' I said. 'What a fucking . . . look at you.'

He went, 'Yeah, I'm lucky to be alive.'

I asked, 'Well what's next? What's the future now?'

'Well,' he said, 'with a lot of physio, I'll be back on the bike as soon as mustard.'

He came third in the senior TT this year.

Streetfighter

I bought this Streetfighter off the internet. The idea behind the whole Streetfighter scene was to take a very quick bike – generally, a four-cylinder in-line motorcycle, like a Suzuki GSX-R1100 – and give it a super-aggressive, sci-fi look. You have to wear a full-face crash helmet with a black visor to complete the look.

So I saw this Streetfighter for sale, and I fell for it when I realized it was a GSX-R1100 Slingshot which had been Streetfightered; it had this crazy rear tail piece with an ostrich and stingray leather seat and this jacked-up rear end, a bespoke exhaust pipe and all that kind of stuff.

For *The Motorbike Show*, we decided to do something completely radical with it: we gave it a six-thousand-quid paint job, powder-coated the frame, changed the bars and, the truth is, we really fucked it up.

We kind of got it a bit wrong. The headlight sticks out too far and the levers don't really quite work with the whole style and ambience of the bike. She's an ugly duckling, but I love her. I spent about fifteen grand on her and she is worth ten, max – because something like that is only worth what someone's prepared to pay for it, and I tell you what, she's an acquired taste.

I can't be arsed to go find somebody who wants to buy her, so, until that time, she sits in my shed.

Chapter 22

Here are some of the things you think as you slide down the A3 at 130 miles per hour, in the prime of your life on a beautiful day:

I'm sliding.

I'm actually ok so far.

I'm going to die.

How long is this going to take to stop?

What am I going to hit?

Speaking of hitting stuff, er, where is the bike?

Oh there it goes! It missed me. Result!

So, really, how long is this going to take to stop?

Eventually, I did stop. And, miracle of miracles, I stood up. Traffic was drawing to a halt around me. Horrified faces at car windows, white with shock, staring. And I, contrary to all expectations, was not just alive, but totally ok.

Thank God I was wearing my leathers. They protected my skin. I wasn't 'degloved', to use the official terminology.

So what the hell was that Alsatian doing there? Who knows, but I didn't have a furry tail sticking out of my crash helmet, so obviously the bloody thing moved.

Since that day, there've been many occasions when I've been riding bikes, all over the world, when an animal has come out of the hedge or has been sitting on the road in front of me. Now I know exactly what to do: aim straight for them. They will move.

*

So despite having had the worst crash of my life, the bike actually kept me alive. Until Guy finally turned up.

By 1988 I'd become something of a recluse. I'd started taking loads of coke, as well as smack, and I didn't want to interact with society at all. I never opened my mailbox because all that was going to bring me was more shit. It was just piling up. The mailbox from hell.

I had a code for the phone: if someone called me, they'd have to give it three rings, ring off and then phone again or I wouldn't answer.

I couldn't even face going out to score. I'd get it all delivered by dispatch riders. I spent seven thousand quid that year on dispatch riders hoofing gear around London for me – that's not including the price of the actual gear, of course. No wonder the company went bust.

Weirdly, the only other people I ever saw were Luke and Matt Goss from Bros. They lived upstairs in another flat in the same building, and, like me, they were quite nocturnal.

Sometimes Brossettes would camp outside the building. I was on the ground floor and I'd open the curtain and then quickly shut it again when I saw them, but they'd all start banging on the window. They'd push a letter under my French windows and say, 'Would you take this up to Matt?'

'No, I fucking wouldn't,' I'd reply, and push it back.

Then, one day, with no Brossettes in residence, I opened the curtains and looked out the French windows and Guy was standing there.

At least, I thought it was Guy. The last time I saw him, he had hair like Jimmy Hendrix, eyes like road maps and he was riding my old GPZ600.

Now, he'd had his hair cut, and he was looking quite plump and red in the face. And he appeared to be riding a bicycle.

I said, 'Guy, is that you? You look like Billy Bunter. Where have you been?'

'I've been in treatment,' he went.

'Oh, right, you can clear off, then.' And I shut the door in his face.

And then I opened it up again. 'You're on a bicycle. What are you doing?'

He said, 'Mate, I'm clean. I've been in treatment down in Weston-super-Mare. Do you want to get clean?'

'Do I fuck, if I'm going to look like you.'

Clunk.

He came round the next day. And the next. He still denies it, but he came round every day for three weeks and eventually I cracked and let him in.

I made a cup of tea.

Then I started crying.

I cried and cried and cried, as I told him what had been going on. It was just awful.

And then he took me to an NA meeting.

Of course, the moment I walked in, I realized where everyone had gone. Half the people there were my mates.

'What are you all doing here?'

'We're all clean, mate. We're trying to get clean.'

'Why didn't you come and see me?'

'We couldn't come and see you, Henry, because you've always got so much gear. We were worried we would end up using.'

I sat and listened for the hour, and at the end I said, 'You're all mad. Higher power? What's all that about? I'll do it my way.'

And off I went.

But Guy kept coming round.

He'd say, 'Come on, mate, let's go to another meeting.'

I sort of knew I was going to have to give this a go because I was so bad, there was no way out.

Funnily enough, one of the things that helped me was my ambition. That was a chink in the junkie armour. There was a definite part of me that thought I could get back into TV if I could get clean.

So I went for it. I lay in bed for a week, feeling as bad as a person ever felt, and Guy came round with other mates of mine who were in recovery, so there was somebody there all the time.

And I got clean.

On 26 August 1988, I went to my first Narcotics Anonymous meeting clean – completely clean of sleepers, methadone, all that kind of shit that I'd bought on the black market. And I went to an NA meeting once or twice a day every day for a year.

I'm three weeks into being clean when my world blows up again. Something I did when I was still using catches up with me.

About two weeks before I had got clean, a bloke I vaguely knew rang me and said, 'Henry, I've got no gear, man, can you get me any?'

'What do you want?'

'I want an eighth of an ounce.'

I said, 'Yeah, I'll get it for you. That's three hundred and twenty-five quid.'

I wasn't a dealer, but I was doing him a favour, so I went off to get it for him.

When he came to collect it, he was with this guy he said was some Mr Big.

So we're having a hoof, and I go, 'Hey, Mr Big,' because I can't remember the geezer's name, 'do you want a hoof?'

'No, I don't take drugs.'

Okie dokie.

About three weeks after getting clean, I wake up to the Brossettes banging on the window: 'Henry, you're front page of the newspaper.'

'Just piss off.'

'No, you are, really, you really are.'

'Really?' So I open the French windows and they thrust the *Sunday People* through.

And yes, I am on the front page: 'HEROIN IN BROS HOUSE.'

And the centre pages: 'HEROIN HENRY, PEDDLER OF DEATH, DEALS DRUGS IN BROS BUILDING.'

Mr Big was actually from the *Sunday People*. And the bastard who brought him round got fifteen grand or something.

I start reading, and it's all like, 'He is the great-nephew

of Gladstone, Britain's most wonderful prime minister, but junkie bastard Henry peddles death from his billion-pound apartment, in a building he shares with the cream of London society, including Luke and Matt from Bros . . .'

And on and on and on it goes.

I'm in shock. I go down to the Chelsea Bun with my friend Sarah. My grey brick mobile starts ringing.

It's my father. And he goes, 'Have you won a television award or something?'

'What makes you say that?'

'Because I've just had your housemaster from Eton on the phone and there's press on the lawn, and they want to know about you.' I say, 'I can't really explain it myself, but go down to Winchester, go into the precinct, get yourself a copy of the *Sunday People*.'

'The Sunday *what*?'

'*Sunday People*. It's a newspaper, Father.'

'All right, I'll call you back.'

I put the phone down and Sarah asks, 'How did that go?'

I say, 'He's gone to get the *Sunday People*.'

She goes, 'Oh, God, really?'

'Well, how else was I going to tell him?'

Twenty minutes later, he phones back. 'You fucking CUNT! I knew you were a wrong 'un! If you think you're going to get so much as five pence off me for the rest of your fucking life, you can think again! You FUCKING SHIT! I bloody well knew it right from the start. As far as I'm concerned, this is the last sentence you're ever going to hear from me. You can fuck off.' Clunk.

And Sarah asks, 'So how did *that* go?'

'Not particularly well.'

So I'm sitting there, thinking my whole life's over.

I'm three weeks clean, I've got a £50,000 overdraft, they're just about to repossess my home. I've got, basically, a sausage bag of clothes to my name.

Then the phone rings again and it's his number.

'Yep?'

He's calmer now.

He says, 'Your mother and I have been talking.'

'Yeah?'

'I've decided that, as you're so far in the shit, I'm going to stand by you.'

And he did.

After not talking to each other in any meaningful way for the whole of our lives, it was quite an amazing thing for him to do. He could quite easily have disowned me, which is what happened to countless mates of mine. But he didn't. He stood by me. He didn't pay off any of my debts, but he supported me emotionally. And it was incredibly important to have his support. In the early days, it helped me to stay clean, because when I was tempted I would think, I can't let the fucker down now.

That moment was the start of my real recovery.

Chapter 23

I got kicked out of the flat, and I moved in with Guy.

He gave me a room in his house – well, actually, I am not sure if 'room' is the correct word, as that typically denotes a space enclosed by four walls and this one only had three and a sheet of really thick plastic where the fourth outside wall was supposed to be.

Still, the rent was cheap.

The first thing I wanted to do when I got sober was to get back into TV. Like I said, I was ambitious – and I think that helped me stay alive.

So I went down to see the old man.

'Father,' says I, 'I want to start a camera-crew business. I want to buy camera gear.'

And he goes, 'How much is it?'

'A hundred grand. I'm going to borrow the money. I was wondering if I could borrow it off you.'

'You've got to save the money, Henry. Typical you; you always want it now.'

'No, Dad, look – it stacks up: the repayments are two grand a month and I make ten grand a month out of the camera kit.'

'No.'

So I went round to a really rich friend of mine – a girl – and told her the story.

She said, 'I tell you what, I'll lend you the hundred grand as long as you, a) pay me back and b) shag me every Sunday.'

Fair enough. Good deal all round, especially as she made a hundred and sixty-two grand back in total.

The World's Best Petrol Can

I love collecting petrol cans. I've got hundreds of them. This 2-gallon petrol can cost me about fifteen quid.

The joy of this particular one was that it had no dents in it. And I saw it and I thought, Well hey, why don't we do the ultimate 2-gallon petrol can?

So I got my mate Stig, who is one of the finest custom painters in the world, to do a custom paint job on it.

He did me a deal and charged me £1000, but he would have charged anyone else £1500 quid. It is the most beautiful thing in my view and it's something that I cherish. I don't really want it for any reason other than I just want the ultimate petrol can, for me, in my shed. And I'm prepared to pay for it.

One day, they'll auction that off and it'll be worth a fortune. Or not. And I don't give a fuck.

I just have this obsession for petrol cans and petrol pumps. And I can't tell you why. Apart from the great thing about collecting petrol cans and petrol pumps, rather than motor vehicles, being that all you've basically got to do as an owner is dust them. So they can accessorize your man cave, and make it look mega retro and cool, but actually, they cost you next to no money whatsoever to own.

And petrol pumps are a good investment. I'll buy one in for five hundred to a grand, do it up and it's worth three grand. So it's an NLE, mate (a nice little earner), although not an SPQR (small profit, quick return).

Petrol cans and pumps are a huge part of automotive history, and if you're going to collect motorcycles and cars, then I think you're going to have to collect the paraphernalia that goes with them. It can only give you another interest – and isn't it great that you can go to an auto jumble and pick up a petrol can?

Also, I'm one of these weirdos who's really knowledgeable about these things, so I feel empowered when I go to an auto jumble that I can find cans that I know are valuable and the person who's flogging them doesn't. And that's really exciting. It's one area that I know really well and I can have one up on someone trying to flog me stuff.

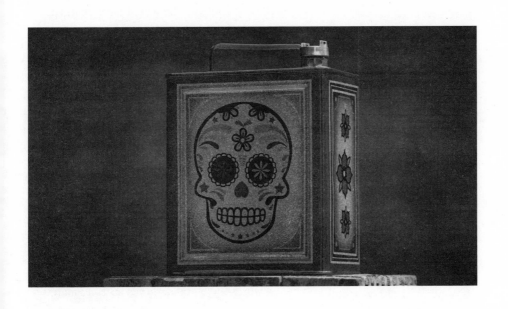

Chapter 24

Now I'm going to have to tell you about the lowest low in my professional life: a movie I directed called *Mad Dogs and Englishmen*.

Unless you are a masochist or a film buff, you'll have never heard of it. The reason for that is because, as the *Guardian* put it in their review, 'It took Roman Polanski six attempts to make the worst film I've ever seen, *Bitter Moon*. Give Henry Cole his due he has succeeded on his first attempt!'

In normal circumstances, a shit film is just a shit film and it doesn't get written about it. Literally thousands of shit films come out every year. You never hear about them, for the very good reason that they are shit. The reason my shit film did get written about, did get ripped apart on the front page of the *Sunday Times*, the *Mail*, Radio Four, you name it, was because, by sheer dumb luck, the star of the movie was one Miss Elizabeth Hurley.

I cast her one afternoon when she was just Elizabeth Hurley – a very, very hot Elizabeth Hurley – and three hours later she wore *that* dress on the *Four Weddings* red carpet, and became the most famous British woman on the planet after Princess Diana.

Good news, right?

No, wrong.

I remember turning to my girlfriend at the time (a model

called Paula Hamilton who, if you are of a certain vintage, you'll remember from her famous Volkswagen ad), the moment she wore that dress and saying, 'That's it. We're screwed.'

But look, I'd better start at the beginning. When I tell the story of *Mad Dogs*, I have to say to people, 'Please, if I'm boring you, tell me to shut up,' because I can still get very emotional about how I was vilified for it, literally strung up in the media like I was Pol Pot.

And I have to remind myself that in the grand scheme of things, it doesn't matter, and 'my terrible experience making a film about my life as a posh junkie' 'ain't exactly losing a limb.

But, that said, let me tell you about the worst year of my life.

Bikes were – as usual – to blame.

This all takes place five years after getting sober – 1993/4. Like I said, I had all this energy I was putting into my career. And in my spare time, I wrote a script about this outsider motorbike dispatch rider – me.

It was really inspired by my GSX-R1100, which I had turned into a rat bike.

Ratting bikes – basically, fucking them up, angle grinding them, spraying them matt black, putting twin crazy headlights on them, covering them in skulls – was a thing. You 'ratted' your bike and you just made it look awful.

There was a school of thought among dispatch riders in the 80s and 90s, that if they really screwed up their bikes, they wouldn't get nicked so often.

The ratting that was going on back then has turned into the whole bike-shed thing now, and of course the rat-rods scene – which is doing the same thing to cars – is massive in America and Europe. It's really cleverly done. It's steampunk on wheels.

Anyway, Guy and all his mates were all pissing around on rat bikes, and so I wrote this dark little movie script about a dispatch rider on his ratted slabside, sprayed matt black with bits hanging off it.

It was after I'd come out of the addiction situation and Straight Face Films had gone bust. I had started this new company, in 1990, with Peter Watson Wood, a glorious old lovie who'd also gone bust. All we had in common was that no one would take our calls, because I was Heroin Henry Peddler of Death and he'd gone down the pan for £3m through no fault of his own – just some investors had pulled out of a movie he was making. Corporate wankers!

So we managed to nick two or three desks and a couple of angle-poise lamps from his old company (Film Screen), carried them across the corridor and set up the new company, Movie Screen.

And there we sat, waiting for the phone to ring.

There were two hopes of getting a job; no hope and Bob Hope, if you know what I mean.

I had my blue and white Gixer, and I couldn't afford to put petrol in it. I was still living with Guy in Battersea, in the room with a plastic sheet for an outside wall, freezing my tits off.

The only work we got was from a mate of mine, Louise Goodman, who used to be the pit-lane commentator on Formula 1 for ITV.

She was an ex-girlfriend and said, 'Look, I know you're in the shit, Henry. I'm working for this PR company and I can give you some videotape duplication – you can mark it up a bit.'

'Nice one, cheers.'

So we were getting videotapes and duplicating them, making like a tenner each.

This went on, until one day, we saw an advert in the back of a broadcast magazine. It said, and I'll never forget it: 'Branch out with TSW! Television South West are looking for a new gardening series.'

I said, 'Peter, you like gardening.'

He goes, 'Do I?'

I went, 'You're fucking right, you do, man. Look, just write a proposal.'

So we wrote a proposal for a show called *Discovering Gardens* and we rang a mate of Peter's, Gyles Brandreth, to see if he would present it.

Anyway, we sent the proposal off without any hope. You're answering an advert in a fucking magazine, you're never going to hear again, are you? But then, one day, TSW rang up and we got the job.

So we started this garden thing – a fourteen-part series with Gyles Brandreth, and then we got a second series and that kind of put us on the map.

We were doing so well we had to move office. I rang John James, who was Paul Raymond's right-hand man.

'John, you got any offices around Soho?'

'Yeah, what do you want?'

'Well I can't really afford a lot, mate.'

'All right,' he went. 'I get your drift. I've got a two-bed flat in Moor Street, if you're interested.'

So, me and Peter went round. John was waiting for us, and there was a door (which is still there today, but it doesn't do what it used to do) with a sign which said, NEW SEXY MODEL SECOND FLOOR.

John asked, 'Do you want to come in, then?'

'I don't know, John. Is there a hooker in it?'

'Yeah, but she's on the second floor. It's the first floor that I want to rent to you.' So we went up this staircase into this pretty all-right two-bed flat with double windows out onto the street and a little balcony.

'Two hundred and fifty quid a week,' said John.

'All right, we'll take it.'

So we spent four years in this two-bed flat, right, with the hookers above us. And it was just the most extraordinary thing living below a brothel, because you were in Soho, but the gay community hadn't come in and made it trendy yet. It was just hookers and the film business and Jeffrey Bearnard in the Coach and Horses getting wasted.

That was it.

We got to know the routines of the hookers, of course. It was New Sexy Model most of the time, which was a couple of birds that were just straight-up sex, but then there was this girl Michelle who did 'interesting and versatile modelling', which meant S&M. She would literally be strapping them to the rack.

Our edit suite, which was the back bedroom, was underneath the rack. Our clients would come in through the door which said New Sexy Model, and then up to the first floor, and I'd say, 'Come and sit with me in the edit suite'. Then suddenly, there'd be this crack of a whip and a groan, and our client would go, 'What the hell? What's that?'

And I'd go, 'Don't worry, it's just some geezer on the rack.'

Every so often, Michelle would come down, fag hanging out of her mouth, and go, 'Are any of you doing anything for five minutes? I'll give you £50 each if you just come up and watch this bloke get lashed. He's one of them that likes being watched.'

So we'd go up and watch this guy who's got a bit in his mouth and a rubber face mask being flagellated with a cat o' nine tails.

Then John James was having work done outside with scaffolding, and so the builders could look through the window, which was even better for Michelle, especially when the builders became clients.

I also got friendly with two undercover cops from the vice squad, Rob and Rob. I gave them keys to our place because they needed to do surveillance on the strip joint opposite that was dealing coke. So you'd come back at eleven at night, dodging the old men coming down the stairs from the brothel, and all the vice squad were in there: 'All right, Henry? How you doing, mate? Do you want a cup of tea?'

It was just the most incredible place to hang out, really. And work was good.

MTV wanted a camera crew every Thursday. Then they also needed one on a Monday or a Tuesday, and suddenly, we were sending out two or three camera crews a day to cover rock and roll.

In the mid- to late 90s, we became *the* rock-and-roll place, and eventually, we had to move out of the New Sex Model building. We moved to Carlisle Street, next door to *Private Eye.*

So my career was going well. I was directing loads of commercials, big ones, I went on tour with bands like N.W.A and Supergrass and we'd accumulated about twenty-five staff.

Chapter 25

Music was a big part of my life as a kid; I used to go ska and punk bands, back in the 70s, when I was fifteen or whatever, although I never saw the Sex Pistols, which I totally regret. For me, they were one of the archetypal bands; there was anger, there was rebellion and there was individualism in that music. But above all there was danger.

Then, in my twenties, music became a huge part of my professional life too.

I spent time on the road with rock bands, and even then, it still felt dangerous, especially when I was filming tours for Public Enemy and N.W.A.

Music is so bland now. There's no danger in it any more. It's all R&B. I feel sorry for my kids having to listen to that shite.

But then it's very, very difficult to get any excitement in anything nowadays. Everyone thinks the internet is the greatest thing ever, but as a parent it's hard to escape the feeling that it's killing all originality.

I say to my boys, 'Listen, why don't you go and *make* the videos that are posted on YouTube? Why don't you ride a BMX bicycle over the roof of that shed and see what happens?'

You're either a human *doing* in this world or you're a human *being*. And as you get older, you realize that you've got to be a human doing when you are young to be able to be a contented human being when you get to my age. Otherwise, you end up one of those sad sixty-year-olds taking coke at dinner parties, trying to be young again. That's really sad.

I don't want to give the impression I was in Public Enemy's inner circle or anything. I mean, I just spent maybe five days living with them and filming them. Flavor Flav – who is the most incredible person ever – wouldn't know me from Adam. But even being around those people for a few days was a real eye opener.

The job came about because I had the contract to supply MTV and VH1 with camera crews, and we ended up being the go-to guys for most of the major record companies. It's like anything; once you're involved in it, people trust you, they know you won't screw it up and they give you more work. So we got a good reputation and we were also editing all these pop and rock videos.

I remember walking into the office one day and seeing all these boxes of footage. 'What is this?' I asked.

'Oh, that's just been sent across by Simon; he needs to cut it.'

I looked at the label.

'Nirvana, eh? Who are they?'

'Oh, they call them grunge.'

So we cut the first live-in-concert for Nirvana. We did stuff for Primal Scream, William Orbit's 'Strange Cargo III' – a lot of abstract stuff. I was clean, but I was living that rock-and-roll lifestyle in a way.

They'd ring up and they'd go, 'David Bowie's playing at the Rainbow, could you get a camera crew down there?'

It was like the news crewing; the majority of the time we just supplied the camera crews who worked for me, but sometimes I'd have to go out on it because either I'd been asked for specifically, I wanted to or there wasn't anyone else in the office.

I'd always do Donington Monsters of Rock, because I loved that – filming or directing; and I also did the Freddie Mercury benefit, which we called the Dead Fred show.

I was on tour with Guns N' Roses – they were just my greatest band of all time, absolutely – and they were coming to do the Dead Fred show.

I remember interviewing Duff, the bassist. He said, 'Is that it, then?'

I said, 'Yeah, yeah, oh, yeah, yeah.'

And he went, 'Ok, man, I just . . . do I have to move?'

And I went, 'Mate, yeah, you do, because we've got to get Slash in here next.'

And he said, 'Man, I'll just like move along the sofa. Because . . . I can't stand up.'

So he moved along the sofa, and Slash came in and sat down.

We started to do the interview with Slash, and halfway through, Duff just got up and said, 'I can walk now.' And off he went to do a soundcheck.

I handed my camera to someone else, followed him out and sat on Duff's bass bin, on stage at Wembley, while he played 'Knockin' On Heaven's Door'.

That was a moment I'll never forget, mainly because Guns N' Roses to me were ethereal. But they were dangerous, they were hardcore. They were proper rockers.

I also spent ten days on the road with Michael Jackson, filming footage for a documentary called *Heal the World*. His nose fell off one afternoon – it literally cracked halfway through the performance.

Mostly what he said to me was, 'Henry, I can't talk. I've got laryngitis.'

I followed him around with a camera, and he could tell whether the lens was zoomed in or it was wide. He was terribly worried that if I zoomed in, I was getting details of his hair and surgery, so he would always go, 'Henry, pull wide, pull wide, pull wide.'

I thought MJ was a nice guy – but it still took nine months to get paid. I remember that.

I think I connected with musicians because, whether you're going to be a rock and roller or whether you're going to have your soul in motorcycling, there's that belief in individualism. With rap music, it's Lamborghinis and cars that bounce up and down, but for me, back in the day, guitar-based rock and roll and motorcycles really came together. We all wanted the same thing: to express ourselves as individuals. So talentless musicians like me could turn to motorcycles to express their individualism.

Uncle Dick Redbeard Gladstone Racer

I hold another land speed record on this beauty; 88.8 miles an hour, which doesn't seem very quick, until you take into account that her engine is from a 350 Triumph, which was a dispatch bike in World War II. It's only supposed to go 30 miles an hour, and the fact that we got it up to nearly 90 is purely down to Sam Lovegrove's talents at tuning a bike.

I actually think it could do more, so we are hoping to take it to Bonneville to get the 350 vintage record. Maybe we can hit the ton.

The bike is named after Uncle Dick Redbeard who instigated the whole thing, of course.

The risk of riding a bike like this at that speed is that all the tolerances are being pushed to the limit. You are running that bike with your finger on the clutch the whole time, waiting for it to nip up. The more you tune a motorcycle, the more it's liable to blow up, and the risk on a bike like this is far greater than running a proper superbike because you're eking out every single tuning possibility to make it go quicker and the engine is seventy years old.

But for me, getting that bike to go at 100 miles an hour is more of a kick than doing 200 on a superbike.

I'm one of these people who loves the vintage situation – the joy of a piece of machinery that has its place in time. What we're actually trying to do is make that period piece of engineering go as quick as it possibly can, and to beat records that have gone down in history over the years, both in the period and since.

No one else around the world gives a fuck; I mean, I hold three vintage land speed records and no one gives a shit. But for us, it's really important – and that's what it's all about, isn't it? It may not make the front page of *MCN*, but it does in my head.

Chapter 26

Anyway, back to *Mad Dogs*. The music work and promo jobs didn't quite do it for Peter, who always wanted to get back in the movies, rather than making these TV shows he didn't quite understand.

'Darling,' he said. 'I really think it's time for you to make a movie. Direct a movie. Why don't you direct a movie? We can put the money together.'

So I went, 'Are you sure? I can direct drama in commercials, but they're fifteen, twenty seconds' worth of drama.'

He said, 'You can do it!'

We had just taken on another guy, Nigel, as a business partner because we had cash-flow problems at the time. Nigel bunged in some money – I can't remember how much – and then something weird happened: Nigel and Peter became these producer lovies together.

Nigel's previous claim to fame was as some kind of political enforcer. He was the geezer who'd taken the poll tax through parliament for Maggie Thatcher and he turned out to be ... well, pretty much what you'd expect someone who got the poll tax through for Maggie Thatcher to be.

So those two are 'developing' this movie, while I'm running around, directing commercials, supplying camera crews to news desks and editing pop promos, Blur and all of that. And I'm working seven days a week – because I'm basically the only person making any money. Then Nigel comes down one day and says he's got some brilliant tax dodge: we're going to finance the movie through the Business Expansion Scheme, the BES, whereby the government give you back 40 per cent of your investment or whatever it was.

So we get an article in the *Mail on Sunday*, and it says we're launching fundraising through the BES for this film about the British aristocracy and Serena Scott Thomas is going to play the lead (because she was a mate of a mate of mine, and she agreed to do it) – and we need just a measly half a million quid to make this movie.

On Monday, we're all sitting there, waiting for the cash to roll in and we get fifteen hundred quid. It's looking like a total disaster, but then, the next weekend, the *Sunday Times* business section do an article – and that Monday morning we have five hundred and sixty grand in the bag.

So, suddenly we're making a movie.

Later that week, Matt, one of my cameramen, calls me.

He says, 'I've just taken a call from this geezer called Ashley. He wants to invest in *Mad Dogs*.'

'Well tell him to just ring the accountant, and it's five hundred quid minimum,' I tell him.

Matt says, 'I told him that, Henry. Do you know what his words were? He said, "What do you think I am, a BT shareholder investor?" I think you should call him.'

So I call Ashley, and he says, 'Henry, I want to invest two million quid.'

'What?'

'I want to invest two million quid. A million quid in a movie and perhaps a million quid for developing other stuff, you know.'

I say, 'Well, you'd better come in and have a meeting.'

So Ashley comes in for a meeting, and he goes, 'I'll give you the million quid on one condition.'

'What?'

'Serena Scott Thomas doesn't play the lead because I think she's shit.'

So we all look at each other and go, 'All right'.

Poor old Serena. That's the way this business goes. She's axed, and he puts a million quid into the pot. And then he gives us another million for development.

Now I have to break the bad news to Serena's agent, Michael Foster. He is renowned, still to this day, as the hardest agent in England.

After I've told Michael's PA that Serena isn't attached to the movie any more, I take a call from Michael. He says, 'Henry, you fucking cunt. I'm going to come round and burn your fucking office down.'

Nothing personal.

And, funnily enough, Michael later represented me.

The good news is, we've now got a total of £1.75 million to make this movie. The bad news is, the script is shocking. I've been madly rewriting it and trying to get it to make some kind of sense, but it's really dark; the basic elements are a bent copper who's shagging his stepdaughter, all this really macabre weird S&M shit, drugs and motorbikes. It's a moody little British movie. Which should have been made for two hundred grand, you know. Slightly out of focus and not really there. Not £1.75 million.

In other terrible news, we've got a rookie script writer, a rookie director, a rookie director of photography and a rookie editor – Simon, who has spent the last year just down the corridor, cutting Supergrass videos and all these pop promos and I'm suddenly telling him he can cut the movie.

Also, we've got no cast. No one to play anything.

I get on the blower to the casting agents, and I get hooked up with this unknown Scottish actor called Ewan McGregor.

I go and sit in some grotty cutting room in Soho and watch the rough cut of a film called *Shallow Grave* – and he's absolutely brilliant.

So Ewan and I meet. And I don't think I've ever met, professionally, such a nice bloke. He turns up on his bike, I'm on my bike, we have the banter, I tell him about the film – that he's playing a dispatch rider – and he goes, 'I'd love to do it. We're on, man. Just do the deal with my agent.'

I say, 'Well, I'll leave all the people to do that and fax each other. As long as you want to do it, brilliant.'

He goes, 'Yeah, man. I love it.'

I'm jumping down the street, thinking, This is amazing. I mean, no one knows who he is, but he's such a top geezer; it's going to be great working with him.

I ring the American distributor, Robbie. 'Robbie,' I go, 'I've got the first person for the film.'

'Who?'

'A guy called Ewan McGregor.'

'Who the fuck is Ewan McGregor?'

'Just wait, right. I've seen this rough cut of this movie *Shallow Grave*, and I think he's going to be mint, yeah, he's new talent.'

'New fucking talent? I don't want any new fucking talent, I want C. Thomas Howell and I've got him, ok, so that's who you're fucking having.'

'Who's C. Thomas Howell?'

'What do you mean? He was in *Soul Man*, *The Hitcher*, you know, man, he's ready to play. And also, he's great for video in the US.'

This was about six weeks before we were due to start filming. So Ewan got ditched. Lucky, lucky guy. I mean, he missed disaster by a fag paper. If he had actually played that film, he probably wouldn't have done *Trainspotting*. I reckon his whole career would have been fucked. It certainly fucked C. Thomas Howell's career, which is some consolation.

Anyway, I'm now lumbered with this American dispatch rider in London. I mean, try working that into your plot.

And we can't find a leading lady. We've been through everyone: Helena, Patsy, Serena. And then Peter goes, 'Well, there's one other.'

'Who?'

'Elizabeth Hurley.'

'Who? Well, let's get her in anyway because we ain't got no one else.'

So Elizabeth Hurley comes in the door and I'll never forget it. Everyone is just knocked out.

She sits down. We get on like a house on fire.

I say, 'Great. You're doing the film.'

I call Robbie in LA. Everyone's happy.

As she's leaving, I say, 'So what are you up to tonight?'

She says, 'Oh, I'm going to the *Four Weddings and a Funeral* premiere.'

'I'll see you there,' I say – because I'm going with Paula.

That evening, we are in the theatre and suddenly, there's absolute pandemonium downstairs.

It's Hurley. With Hugh Grant. And she is wearing that safety-pin dress. Overnight, she becomes a household name.

Overnight.

For that dress.

And I've just cast her three hours earlier for *Mad Dogs*.

I turn to Paula and I say, 'I'll tell you right now – our movie's not going to be the same.'

Next morning, sure enough, when LA wakes up, I get a phone call from Robbie.

'Man, you're a fucking genius, dude!'

'Robbie, I'm not so sure—'

'Fuck that, man. This is how it's going to roll. Just forget the word, "dark", ok. Forget the word "British". Forget the word "indie". You can remember the word "film" or "movie", as we like to call it here. Just think, "commercial movie of the week". Get rid of all the dark shit, man. Get rid of everything in the script that's weird.'

'Robbie, I can't.'

'Fucking do it, man. Remember, I have cut approval, so you might as well do it now.'

So with just three weeks to go until shooting, every single bit of darkness in the film is taken out.

I've managed to get Joss Ackland as the copper, and then C. Thomas Howell turns up from America, looking like someone out of Bros – ripped jeans, red baseball cap.

Day one of filming finally arrives, and we prepare to shoot the first scene. My first ever movie scene.

Hurley has just been raped by Joss Ackland, and C. Thomas Howell, who's having an affair with her, comes to the hospital to find out what's happened. Hurley is in bed, covered in blood, and C. Thomas Howell is coming down the corridor.

I can already tell there's something wrong just by doing the sequence of him running through the corridor. And then he comes in to see her. Slate one, take one:

'Oh, my GOD! What's happened to you?'

I shout: 'Cut. CT, look, I'm new to this, but I've got to tell you, I think less is more, mate. Why don't you come in and just stare at her? I mean, forgive me.'

'Yeah, got it, got it, got it.'

'Ok, slate one, take two.'

'Oh, my GOD . . . sorry, what do you want me to do?'

'Cut.'

We get to slate nine and I haven't even got him sitting by the bed yet. This scene is so fucking atrocious, and it sets the tone for the whole film.

There are situations in life where you've got to be bold, and not take any shit, but I was so complicit then that I would compromise very quickly.

Nowadays, I would tell the cameraman, 'Mate, if you fucking hassle me one more time, I'll punch your fucking lights out. I'm doing this close-up whether you like it or not. I don't give a fuck.' But back then, I was learning on the job. With 120 crew. It was insane.

And it didn't help that I was rewriting the script as we went along.

I had a scene where a motorcyclist gets machine-gunned down. Spent twenty-five thousand quid in a day doing that. And never used it because it didn't quite work because the script was only half written when I did it.

Anyway, we stagger on to the end of this terrible movie. Then we have to watch a rough cut, and it's just so awful. I mean, not just bad – it's total shit.

We cut it together into some kind of shape and we get the cast and crew down to the Chelsea cinema to watch it.

I get up and I say, 'Well this is it. I don't know how happy I am with it, but this is it. I hope you enjoy it. Thank you for all your hard work, off we go.'

An hour into the film, the fire alarm goes off and all the lights come on.

A bloke from the cinema comes in and says, 'You're all going to have to leave. I'm so sorry, it's a fire alarm.'

So 350 of us pile out onto the King's Road until the all-clear is given. But when we go back in, three-quarters of the audience have gone home.

And they were cast and crew!

Two weeks later, we meet Nigel, from the UK distributor. He's a nice bloke, all upbeat. He says, 'So, when's the premiere?'

Left: Up to mischief in my tails at Eton in 1978 with mates Dave and Ed.

Below: At Eton in 1979 – my Two Tone phase.

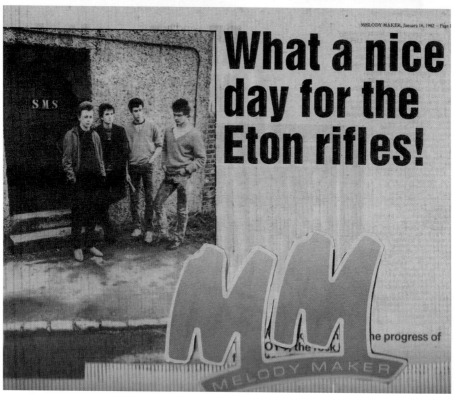

MELODY MAKER, January 16, 1982 – Page 1

What a nice day for the Eton rifles!

SMS

the progress of

MELODY MAKER

Melody Maker article on my band Tannoy 7. We thought we'd made it – how wrong we were!

Five years on the heroin between 1983 & 1988 took its toll both personally and publically. Now 30 years clean of drugs and drink I still feel the consequences but I'm one of the lucky ones who survived it ... Fuck knows how!

THE **People**

September 4, 1988 . No.5557(P)   FORWARD WITH BRITAIN   35p ★L

EXPOSED!

HEROIN DEALER IN BROS HOUSE

IDOL: Luke

Danger for pop idol's teeny fans

BROS star Luke Goss is living in the same house as a dangerous heroin dealer.

● The two men often chat with one another, even though they occupy separate flats in the luxury building in West London. Crowds of impressionable young fans are constantly hanging around outside while Henry Cole pushes drugs inside.

● Many of the youngsters spend hours waiting for a glimpse of their idol — only yards from where the peddlar of death plies his evil trade.

Full story — Centre Pages

Neighbours Exclusive

CHARLENE IN SEX SCANDAL

See Pages 12 and 13

PLUS . . . Go to Australia and meet the stars

PLUS

'Reggie pushed the knife into his face...he stabbed his stomach and chest and impaled him through the throat to the floor... **He was dead**'

THE **TRUE** STORY OF THE EVIL KRAYS...ONLY IN THE **People**

Filming and directing the movie *Mad Dogs and Englishmen* in 1994. It turned out to be one of the most challenging experiences of my life but the poster was cool …

Stars and Cars – my first presenting gig for Channel 5 back in 1996. It ran for five years and opened up the chance to put bikes on TV …

Riding Route 66 in 2000 was the first bike show for Travel Channel. Riding "The Mother Road" was a life-changer and led to *World's Greatest Motorcycle Rides* that, eighteen years later, is on series 23!

Riding in New Zealand. There isn't a straight road – fantastic!

Left: South Africa – if you're into dual sport it's the best.

Above: Nullarbor Plain, Australia. You haven't experienced loneliness on a bike until you've ridden this – a 2500 mile road of nothing. Somewhere to find yourself?

Straight line racing is my only drug now. Setting a land speed record at Bonneville Salt Flats, riding a Brough Superior, in 2013 was a highlight.

Setting a British record for a 350 on our Gladstone "Red Beard" racer. No drug beats the feeling of going as fast as you can – believe me I've tried them!

Right: *Shed and Buried* TV series with Sam Lovegrove. The nicest, most talented and gifted hippy you'll ever meet!

Right: *Find It Fix It Flog It* for Channel 4 with my great mate Simon O'Brien – more shed dwelling. Nowhere else I would rather be except riding a bike!

Below: Filming for *The Motorbike Show* for ITV4 has its risks. Here I am at Watford A&E with stuntman Richie who I was trying to copy – broke my shoulder in three places. Twat!

My wife Janie and I heading out in the Willys Jeep.

Our boys Charlie and Tom living it up on my 1968 Russian sidecar outfit.

The family dressed up at Salon Privé Concours on the Gladstone stand.

There's just silence. And Julie, the PR woman, goes, 'Have you seen the film, Nigel?'

He goes, 'No, no. I only ever see the films at the premieres.'

'We're not having a premiere.'

'Why not?'

'Because the film's shit.'

I pipe up: 'I am actually sitting here, you know.'

She says, 'Henry, I'm just telling him the truth. The film is shit. It's going to get ripped apart. Don't have a fucking premiere.'

So on the Thursday night of release, it came out on about twenty screens UK-wide.

Cue my moment of fame in the *Guardian* film pages.

But the problem was, the reviews weren't where they normally were. They were on the front pages because of Elizabeth.

Anyway, on the Monday morning I went to the office feeling quite bullish, and I rang my agent, Ian Wilson (who used to be Bruce Forsyth's agent), and I said, 'Ian, what's happening mate? I'm feeling up for it.'

He said, 'Well there are nineteen offers today of different shows to go on to justify why you made *Mad Dogs* – and you're not doing any of them.'

'What? Why not?'

'Henry, just go on holiday, yeah. Don't even try to get involved. They have got their knives out for you, for Elizabeth, for the whole thing. Just forget it.'

I rang my mate Simon. 'Come to Prague,' I said.

We were in the cab on the way to Heathrow when *LBC Movie Week* started up on the radio. 'Today, we'll be reviewing the, ah, concerning movie, shall we call it, *Mad Dogs and Englishmen ...*' All the panel are laughing. '... we did invite the director, Henry Cole, to be on the show, but ...'

I leaned forward to the cabbie and said, 'Switch that shit off, mate, will you?'

The movie had wrecked my life for a year, but the funny thing was, Ian was right. I went to Prague, and after a week, I came back, and as far as everyone was concerned, apart from taking the piss out of me, none of it had happened. That was the most incredible lesson learned in all of it.

The incredible thing that came out of all that shit is my friendship with Elizabeth Hurley, who has since stood by me as a dear friend. I've yet to get her on a motorbike, but her loyalty, support and often disbelief at my antics is never-ending and she's godmother to my youngest, Tom.

In all the bollocks of A-list celebrities, she is a shining example of someone who is real, grounded and genuine. She has quietly helped to raise over $160m for breast cancer over the years. Need I say more?

As for failure – it tells you that you mustn't stop trying, you've got to give it a go, whatever the outcome might be. It's the same in recovery. You've got to try your hardest, but let go of the result. Because all that matters, when you reach those depths, is that you've done your best for you, at the point of life that you're at.

I was twenty-eight. I was five years clean and I didn't have a clue. When people would interview me on set, and ask what's your favourite movie, I'd say, *Lethal Weapon* and *Wayne's World*. I didn't know you weren't supposed to say that.

Failure is a wonderful thing, if you understand why it's so important. Every single person who I have a real connection with has had problems: it could be illness, it could be a business that flopped, it could be drugs, it could be parents dying early. It could be they've really fought for it, yeah, and lost, failed, but not given up.

I have lots of regrets about that film, but the really amazing thing about *Mad Dogs* was that I had to pick myself up and carry on.

Chapter 27

The other thing that combined with the disaster of *Mad Dogs* was the debacle of my personal life.

When I was about three or four years clean, I used to go out sharking with my mates Si and Ronnie, giving it large in Ronnie's Porsche.

Ronnie was a top geezer, a bald Cypriot wild boy, who sold telecoms in the City. We'd all pile into his car, put the roof down and cruise the King's Road.

Ronnie, typical salesman, had this tactic of chatting birds up that I just couldn't believe. He'd go past a bus stop, see a beautiful girl and slam the brakes on. Then he'd get out of the car, and he'd go, 'Emma, I haven't seen you for twenty years! I can't believe it's you.'

And obviously she'd go, 'I'm not Emma'.

Then he'd act all crestfallen and say, 'I'm so sorry! She was the love of my life! And she was the most beautiful woman I've ever seen – and now I see you.'

He did it all the time, and probably 50 per cent of times he got a result. Classic Chelsea wide-boy stuff.

Anyway, Ronnie had a flat on Hyde Park Gate, and Si and I turned up there one day because we were all going to a party down in Wandsworth.

We walked in and Ronnie was in his uniform of Armani suit and white shirt.

'All right, Ron?' I said, and then I turned to my right, where this girl was sitting on the sofa. And I literally went to jelly.

I was wearing blue and white cowboy boots with eagles on them. I had the long hair, but no beard; it was basically 90s heathen-chic.

She had an Alice band and a necklace.

I went, 'Hi, I'm Henry. This is Si.' My voice was all wobbly.

And she went, 'Oh, hello. I'm Janie.'

I was just thinking, You're gorgeous, and I'm worried I'm about to lose it. So I went into the kitchen and Si said, 'You fancy her, don't you?'

I went, 'She's gorgeous, man.'

He said, 'Shall I give you a prophecy?'

'Oh, fuck off, one of your prophecies,' I said. 'You're always giving me prophesies.'

He said, 'You're going to marry her.'

'Fuck off. She's nobbing Ronnie.'

'No she ain't.'

Anyway, after a bit, we all headed off to this guy called Roland's party in Wandsworth. I was sitting on this wrought-iron bench in the garden and she was sitting right next to me, and I knew I had to make my move.

So I thought I'd do the hand trick. This is where you put your hand a bit close to her leg, uncomfortably close, but you're not actually doing anything. You have plausible deniability.

And then, you know, if she doesn't move her leg, you can maybe give it a little stroke.

Anyway, I go for the stroke and she puts her hand on mine. Result!

I said, 'Are you and Ronnie—'

'Oh, God, no,' she said. 'He's just a friend.'

And that's how Janie and I started dating.

Janie was living in Battersea with her mate Johnny. Then one day she said, 'Why don't you come and live with me?'

I went, 'Really?'

'Yes,' she went.

So I moved out of the room with a plastic sheet for a wall and I moved in with Janie and Johnny. Everything was going great – a year, you know, a year and a half; it's all good.

But I had one massive issue that was unresolved.

I really, really wanted to be famous.

I hear kids these days saying, 'I want to be famous', and I think, You poor, stupid sods, you really don't. But then I have to be honest with myself and say that, at that time in my life, I desperately wanted to be acknowledged in some way, and I didn't understand how all that stuff just doesn't matter.

I was working on a celebrity TV programme called *The Restaurant Show* for ITV, and the first episode was about a flying Indian restaurant over London. The idea was you get in this Cessna and eat as you fly over the capital. It was clearly a truly terrible idea – I'd been in enough Cessnas in my news-crewing days, snaking with the wind, to know you would not feel like eating an Indian entrée in one of them. But I faithfully turned up to Biggin Hill airfield, and it turned out the celebrity we were doing was Paula Hamilton.

So Paula came on to me, and I went back to my old ways, didn't I, and I walked out on Janie.

Paula and I started to get involved, and you want to know what I really saw in that woman? A chance to get a slice of her fame: the film premieres, *Hello!* magazine, all that shite.

I genuinely thought I'd made it.

She made me have my hair cut, she made me smarten up my act completely and then she started taking me out with her.

The paparazzi, initially, were all excited about Paula's new man, you know, *film director Henry Cole.*

I liked that. But then, after a while, they started saying, 'Oh, Henry, can you just stand back a bit?' And they'd take a photo of her on her own, and I started to feel even more hollow inside and more awful than before.

Slowly, I realized that the dream that I thought was there – fame, glamour, premieres – was just bollocks.

Fame is actually a pretty awful thing, if, like her, you're really only famous for one TV commercial as opposed to being famous for being or doing something outstanding.

And I learned that the loneliness of it – the emptiness you feel when you are worried someone is not taking your photo – is just the most overwhelming and terrible sort you can experience. It is a special type of hopelessness – the hopelessness of wanting the world to know you when the world doesn't care.

Why did I want that? Why did I want to walk into a restaurant and have people know who I am? Why did I think that would fulfil me?

I think I missed the biggest red flag of all when, as part of the general, *Hello!*-ready smartening-up exercise, I made the decision to get rid of my motorcycles. They didn't fit with the fame game that Paula was a part of, and that I was so pathetically trying to grab a slice of. I was chasing this dream, you know.

The moment I stopped going down to Chelsea Bridge on a Friday night, I truly stopped being me. I had gone and destroyed the two things I loved so much and meant everything to me: Janie and my motorcycles. What a total twat I was.

There could hardly be a more symbolic image of how much I hated myself, and how lost I was, than selling my bikes. It was a rejection of my whole past, my whole existence to that point.

No wonder I really bought into the narrative of the press after *Mad Dogs*: 'Henry Cole, what a fucking loser.'

I tried to reinvent myself with nicely quiffed hair and products from Jo Malone. Not having motorcycling in my life was a statement of how badly my life had gone off the rails. How wrong it had all gone.

The nadir of our relationship came after we had split up.

My agent rang up and told me I could make fifteen grand if I went and opened a dogs' home in Marbella for the marquesa, owner of *Hello!* magazine.

What?

'It's her pet project. She wants you and Paula, as a couple getting back together again, to go and do it.'

So I got on the plane, did this thing and earned my fifteen

grand. Paula and I took separate planes on the way home. It was crap celebrity shit, big time.

And then the terrible, terrible realization that I had left Janie for this bogus dream descended on me.

I loved Janie to bits.

I was the world's biggest idiot. I dumped the love of my life for Paula.

I was straight, I was clean, but I had this emptiness inside me still.

I didn't understand what contentment meant or even looked like.

I truly hit rock bottom.

CJ2A Willys Jeep

Like all my best restos, I found this in a shed. It's a CJ2A Willys jeep, built in 1947, so it's representative of this really interesting time, just after WWII, when so many vehicles that had established themselves in the war and done good business as military vehicles were trying to find their place in civilian life.

The Willys jeep was an iconically American machine – over half a million were made for the war effort – but the story goes that they were based on an illicit breakdown of the British Land Rover somewhere in the Scottish Highlands. And you definitely feel the Land Rover in its DNA.

This truck was built as civilian, with bigger headlights, a different gear box, and different price. If it was World War II, it would be worth £25,000, but because it's 1947 it's worth about £15,000.

Just the other day, I put a new sidelight on it. (It never had one on one side.) I worked out the wiring, made a new bit of the loom for it, I put the light in and made a little bracket to put it on – and I switched it on, and the thing worked.

Now, let me tell you, the headlights went out shortly afterwards, and if that ain't a metaphor for life I don't know what is.

But the point is, I got a kick from doing it, and doing it nice and slowly. Restoration cannot be rushed; if you do rush it, you're missing the whole point of what it's all about. It's nothing to do with the finished project. In fact, finishing is quite a depressing moment because the motor you've lived with for a year, that you've been restoring – suddenly it's done and you think, Oh, what happens now?

At the end of the day, the fun is in the resto.

Also, you cannot cut corners. The minute you say, 'Actually, I can't be arsed to do that side light, and no one will notice anyway' – that is the moment that the project is over and you might as well just stick the thing on eBay for free collection. Yes, you are right, no one will notice, but when you start cutting corners you are not engaged with the restoration and you have bodged it and that lack of finish and attention to detail will spread to the whole of the rest of the project.

It's like graffiti. If there's one tiny bit of graffiti on a wall in a town, within a week that wall will be covered in it.

And that is the epitome of life, isn't it? Sums it up. The minute you start bodging your relationship or your career, it's over, mate.

Chapter 28

This all happened during the run-up to *Mad Dogs* and the filming of it. Janie wasn't with me when I made it. If she had been, it would have been a very different film.

My mate Sebastian Rich, the legendary war cameraman, had never been happy about me splitting with Janie.

'What the fuck are you doing, Henry? Why are you hanging out with Paula?' he said one day.

'I don't know, mate,' I said.

'Get back to Janie.'

'Oh fuck off, Seb,' I went.

He said, 'Look, right, I ain't going to speak to you while you're with Paula. But every Friday I'll phone you. That's the only time I'll speak to you, and I'll say, "Do you want to be picked up yet?" And you just tell me "Yes" or "No" and then I'll put the phone down, right?'

And sure enough, every Friday for nine months he rang me, and every Friday I went, 'Fuck off, Seb'.

Then one Friday night, he rang up and said, as usual, 'Do you want to be picked up?'

And I very quietly went, 'Yes. Please.'

He was there twenty minutes later.

All I thought about for the next few months was how I was going to get back with Janie.

I finally met Johnny – Janie's flatmate – at a party and he gave me the encouragement I needed to contact Janie again.

I literally begged her forgiveness and, thank God, she gave me a second chance.

Unfortunately, I am one of those twats who has to lose something before they realize how precious it is. With Janie, miraculously, I was able to find it again.

We got married pretty soon after that.

Janie's parents are amazing.

Her dad, David Coombes, is, I think, the coolest guy I've ever met. He was a tailor in Savile Row, and he made all the suits for anyone who was anyone in the '60s. He did the suits for *The Prisoner*, for *Get Carter*, for all those movies.

When I met him in the early 90s, he had a clientele of the richest Americans. These billionaires would fly over in their private jets, and have him make him ten suits. And to this day, they're still ringing him, at eighty-three, asking if he'll make them a suit.

He was a bad boy himself, and I think that's why he gave me a second chance.

It was Janie's mum, Pam, who was working in the film industry in Wardour Street, who tamed him.

Me and Janie were like history repeating itself. You can, of course, imagine that people were warning him off me, because I was a bad boy, but he welcomed me into his home – and then I ran off.

Then, a year later, she said to him, 'I'm taking Henry back.'

Now, no normal parent would go, 'Well yeah. Give him a run.' But he did. Because he understood two things. Firstly, he knew that Janie was still in love with me – he saw the pain and anguish and the two stone that she had lost. Secondly, he knew from his own experience that, yes, some of us bad boys can be tamed.

So I'm in love with my wife, but I'm also in love with my in-laws.

Without them it would have been very, very difficult for us to be who we are today. It probably wouldn't have happened.

My dad checked out long ago, and my mother takes quite an evasive approach to life's problems: 'Oh, well, never mind darling. It'll be ok. Do you want a slice of cake?'

My father-in-law, on the other hand, goes, 'Look, you twat, what are you doing?' or 'No, I don't think you should do that, I think you should do this.'

I've taken his advice on many, many occasions – and it's always worked.

Chapter 29

It's weird – out of all the women I had relationships with, I never really came close, I don't think, to properly finding the right one before I met Janie.

It's a very difficult thing, to find your right partner, your soulmate, and relationships kept not working out for me because I was always getting involved with people whose careers were almost as overriding as my own.

We would always fight over who was the most tired, who was under the most pressure, who needed the sympathy.

But Janie's a very special person. And I still fancy her rotten after however many years since we first met in 1992, which is the key to a long-term relationship, isn't it?

Because, if you don't fancy that person any more, really there's not much hope is there? I mean, I could just marry Hamish, my MD, right? Or Ben, the production manager upstairs, if I didn't have to sleep with them.

When you see your wife come downstairs to go to a party, you've still got to think, even twenty-five years on, 'Shit, man, I don't want to be taking anyone else to that party. She looks a picture.' And as she gets older, she gets better looking. Better and better.

(I'd like to point out here that if I did fancy Hamish, I'd definitely marry him – if he'd have me. I've never understood what the Church has against gay marriage. Aren't they supposed to encompass and embrace everybody? Who are those people out there who still believe that you cannot have gay marriages? What is that about? If you are lucky enough to find someone you're truly in love with, whoever they may be, whatever their sexual orientation, there should be a loving Church that says, 'Come on in'. I know things are changing, but it is incredible it has taken so long. This world is tough, man, and if you fall in love, you are super lucky, and it really does not matter who you fall in love with, as long as that's someone who really cares for you, deep down.)

So Janie gets constant abuse from me about the broccoli, but at the end of the day she's only offering me broccoli because she really cares about our future together.

Relationships are crazy. Of course, you can buy your wife a new car to keep the peace, right, or she can get you a new shed for Christmas, but all that's nothing compared to when you find a note in your bag that says, 'I miss you'.

These are the rules in our household: anything to do with the children or the house, Janie has final say, right; anything to do with what goes on in the sheds, the garden, outside, I have final say.

We had a new kitchen put in recently, and I didn't even know what it looked like until it had been fitted. I didn't need to, because I trust her and whatever makes her happy makes me happy too.

We trust each other. I go off round the world all the time and I wouldn't even have a sniff at somebody else and I know she wouldn't either.

If I was caught in bed with a small gerbil or something, then I'd give her half straight away. There would be no argument. We'd just sell the lot and we'd go fifty-fifty – because I couldn't have done any of this or got through all the shit that I've been through without her. It's just impossible. I'd probably have gone off the rails at some point and I definitely wouldn't be writing this now.

I only feel insecure when I'm feeling shit about myself. When I was diagnosed with diabetes, I genuinely thought, Why would she stay with me? I'm vulnerable now; I'm not big old Henry. I've got hardly any teeth because of my heroin abuse thirty years ago and I'm waiting for my implants to be done. So why would she want to be with me?

But when I'm in a good place with my self-worth, I think, Well she wants to be with me, perhaps, because she still might fancy me from a distance and, you know, I'm quite a nice geezer, really. I don't have any skeletons in the cupboard. I'm just a regular bloke.

What I've learned about my relationships with other people is that, ultimately, they are dependent on my relationship with myself.

Honda Cub

The Honda Cub is an extraordinary part of history and I think every self-respecting motorcyclist should have one in the shed because it was the vehicle that gave mass populations the ability to move around. It was developed for the Asian market by Honda, and the design brief was for a moped you could take the whole family on, not just one other person.

You can ride it with one hand, this beautiful little twist-and-go moped that cruises along at 30. It's super easy to ride, and to this day, over 100 million of them have been made. It's the most prolific motorcycle ever.

It is responsible for everything in Asia. Without the C50 Cub Moped, no one would get around.

Here, they were the quintessential commuter bike, with the granny faring on, the leg-guards and that kind of stuff, you know.

The Cub is the ideal learner bike. It's a rite of passage for everyone. You've got to start somewhere and a C50 Cub Moped is the place to do that. The great thing about it is you don't have to worry about changing gears, which is generally one of the most difficult things for someone starting off riding a motorcycle.

But most important to me is that it's the last motorcycle that my mother rode with me, when she was eighty-eight. She sat on the back and I'd take her round the paddock and down the road on it. And consequently, I'll never sell it.

It's everything that a motorcycle should be, in the sense that it's a vehicle you can share with your nearest and dearest – and now my kids are riding it. It's just great to see them do that. And all this has happened on a motorcycle that cost seven hundred quid.

Chapter 30

After *Mad Dogs*, it's fair to say my prospects were not particularly bright vis-à-vis the making of feature films.

I thought I was going to be a movie director and do a film called *Living Evidence* with Michael Caine. I was all set up to do it, but they pulled the plug after *Mad Dogs*.

To be honest, I'd have been happy at that point to go and retire to a shed somewhere in the West Country and ride my bike to the shops every day to get a pint of milk and a packet of biscuits. And that's probably what I would have done, had I not had twenty-five staff.

But I did, and I had to feed that pony. All those people had come to work for me in good faith and I had a duty to make sure they were ok.

So I was ringing everyone looking for work, pitching ideas. I'd ring places like the BBC and the commissioning editor's receptionist would say, 'I'm sorry, there's really no point in me putting you through, Henry, is there?'

But one guy who did take my call was William Campbell, the CEO of Playboy TV worldwide.

He was possibly as desperate as I was to speak to somebody, and he agreed to a meeting.

'What's the address?' I asked, imagining it would be some glass-fronted edifice on Piccadilly where the Playboy club used to be.

Not quite. Try Hayes. The street name – and you couldn't make this up – was Pump Lane.

I went down to Hayes on the bike one afternoon, and probably I was the only person involved in TV who had ever done that, and William and I hit it off.

We sat in his very unglamorous office, laughing and joking about life in general and, more specifically, my disastrous efforts to make it in the world of film. Then William said, 'Well, look, we're really looking for some early-evening documentaries, pre-watershed, for Playboy TV UK.'

Any good proposal that I've ever come up with, I've either thought about while washing my hair in the shower or absolutely on the spur of the moment. I've never, ever got a production away where I've written out a proposal and researched it for three months.

'Well,' I said, 'why don't we do something like Eurotrash? Going round different cities, checking out the adult entertainment scene?'

'Maybe . . .'

'We could call it the *Sex Guides*. And we could go round and do a review of adult entertainment in each city around Europe.'

'Actually, yeah, great,' William said. 'Why don't we do that?'

'I've got this idea of doing a sort of lunatic, comedy voiceover for it.'

'Great, I love it.'

'Really?' I asked

He went, 'Yeah, ok. Give me fourteen half hours.'

'Really?'

'Yeah,' said William. 'I need it.'

So I went, 'All right. So, what's the bad news on the budget?'

He hesitated. 'Yeah, it is quite bad. How did you guess?'

'Well, how bad?'

'Eight grand a half hour.'

Eight grand is about as close to nothing as you can get to make a show involving travel. But I had nothing else on, so I said we'd do it.

My producer, Jonah, and I, we set off on this unbelievable, extraordinary journey across Europe. Six weeks we were on the road. And I immersed myself in a subculture of sex work, that of course I'd known, intellectually, was out there, but had never experienced.

As a news cameraman, you become a bit desensitized, as I said before. You see a dead body, and to get you through it, you make a joke about it or ignore it. It's horrific, but essential in enabling you to cope. And we ended up doing the same thing when we were filming sex workers and sex shows every night.

We started off in Amsterdam at the Casa Rosso. What they do there is pretty simple; a man and a woman shag on a revolving bed, while fifty Japanese tourists sit and watch them. There's also a warm-up gig, which is a masturbating gorilla. They say, 'Please put your hands together for the randy monkey,' and on comes this bloke in a monkey suit who gets his todger out. Not a real todger, but a plastic one – from which he then sprays milk on the Japanese tourists.

Nice.

Next up were the two people who just shagged on stage, and did everything you could possibly imagine.

So we were filming them backstage when I picked up a camera, put my back out and couldn't move.

It just so happened that the woman who was shagging onstage was a chiropractor in her day job. So after she came off, she came over to help me.

She told me to lie on my back and put my legs in the air, but she was treating me totally naked. And she had these love beads still hanging out of her.

She said, 'Oh, these are really uncomfortable. Will you pull them out? I can't reach them.'

'Er, ok.'

Hence the desensitization around everything that went on with the *Sex Guides*.

We went deep down into this subculture. We became like them: sleeping by day and working by night. We went on porn sets, to lap-dancing bars, brothels – all these places, all over Europe.

We would literally turn up and go, 'Hi, We're from Playboy TV would you mind if we filmed you?'

Weirdly, most people said yes.

The Germans were the craziest.

They just loved their S&M.

At that time in Germany there were two types of places where you could pay for sex.

The first was disused tower blocks called Eros Centres, which used to be one-bed council flats, but all of which were now brothels. They were all legal and in every major city in Germany. You went in, you paid your entry fee and then you had all these hookers in different apartments to choose from.

The other place you could go for paid sex in Germany was on industrial estates – past the plumbing parts wholesaler and welding supplies and all that, and then you get to this one industrial building which is an S&M parlour.

One time, we were interviewing a dominatrix in one of these industrial estates and after about twenty minutes she said, 'Sorry, I have to stop the interview. I have a client.'

'Ok,' I said, 'well, we'll get out.'

'No, no, he's here.'

'What do you mean he's here?'

And she got up, went behind this curtain and came back pulling this naked guy along the floor, with a bit in his mouth, trussed up in the foetal position. He'd been there all along, not a word out of him.

Then she put him back behind the curtain and carried on the interview.

We once turned up at a place in Prague and a cleaner said, 'Ah, it's finished. We are closed for ever now.'

'Why did you close?' I asked.

'Oh, the boss, he did not like his wife. He cut her up into pieces, threw her in the river. He has been arrested.'

Another time, in Brussels, we were at a strip joint, and the bloke said, 'Ja, you film in here as much as you want. But you have to leave by nine o'clock.'

'All right. But why nine o'clock?'

'That's when all the MEPs come in,' he explained. 'They won't want to be filmed.'

The sex club subculture was reminiscent of the biking subculture, and we were completely accepted by the people involved in it because we weren't arrogant. We didn't believe we were above them, and that helped us to gain their trust, to get in and film them, which we managed to do on a nightly basis.

I think I just connect with people who, for whatever reason, don't fit in.

I never partook of the goods – I was back with Janie by this time, and she trusted me to go off and make these films – but I actually felt quite at home.

And the shows were great, and the money kept the doors open.

But the icing on the cake was when I went to the Cannes TV Festival and Playboy America came up to me and said, 'Henry, man, did you make the *Sex Guides*?'

I went, 'Yeah. But don't tell anyone, because we all had fake credits.'

They said, 'We love it, man. We want to buy it for America. How does $35,000 sound to you?'

I went, 'Bang on, man, happy days, son.'

Thirty-five thousand dollars for fourteen shows we'd already made? Why not.

Two weeks later, the contract from the Americans came through. It was $35,000 per episode – thirty-five times fourteen, which just about paid off the debts we were left with after *Mad Dogs*.

Chapter 31

I ended up doing another job for Playboy TV – twenty five-minute interviews with the Playmates. Janie knew I wouldn't touch any of them. You're much more likely to touch someone in the accounts department at the Christmas party, to be honest.

On my first shoot with a Playmate, I said, 'Darling, look, I wonder whether there's any chance of you just undoing another button of your blouse and just sexually putting your hand into your breast and just rubbing your breast like that. Would that be at all possible?'

She looked at me, and asked, 'What do you want me to do again?'

By the end it was: 'Right. Next sequence. Just open your blouse right down to your navel, right, get your hand in and rub your tits, ok, but do it sexily. Right, rolling, do it.'

Much easier.

Hamish – who is now my managing director – started working for me on those shoots as a work-experience kid. All the promos we did were for transmission before the watershed, so if a nipple popped out without anyone noticing and got into the footage, it was a disaster.

But it kept happening because I wasn't focused on the woman's nipple. I was interested in getting the look and the style of her performance. That might sound ridiculous over a Playboy promo, but it's true.

So someone had to be on nipple watch.

I said to Hamish, 'Hamish, this is your work experience. I want you to sit on that stool there, and if you see a nipple come out, just shout, 'Nipple!' That's all you've got to do.'

He went, 'Oh, right. Ok.'

And so every so often there was a shout of, 'Nipple!' and we'd have to cut.

After the work experience that day, I said to the camera crew, 'So what's the new boy like?'

And they said, 'He's a really lovely bloke.'

At the end of the day, Hamish came up to me and he said, 'Can I have a job now?'

I went, 'What are you talking about? You're twelve.'

He said, 'Well, I'm actually eighteen. I'm going to university. But can I have a job when I finish?'

Just to get rid of him, I said, 'Well, yeah, whatever, mate, of course you can.'

And then three years later he rang me up.

'Hamish?' I went. 'Who the fuck are you?'

'You promised me a job,' he said.

'Oh God, you're Nina's brother. All right, then. Start Monday.'

That was about twenty years ago and he's managing director now. He runs everything. I just do what he says.

Partnerships are a weird thing. The partnerships that have worked for me in love and in business have been where the two partners want different things out of the relationship.

For me and Janie, we work because I'm a workaholic and she ain't. We have very different attributes and the perfect relationship is where two people can bring those different attributes together to make a glorious whole.

A partnership in the TV business only works, in my view, if one is the nuts and bolts: 'Here's the cash flow; we've got twenty grand in the account,' and that's what I have Hamish for. He is a brilliant business man and unflappable – me, on the other hand, I'm the exact opposite and that's why our relationship works.

When you choose to work in TV you live it, you breathe it and, if you don't, you'll fail in it. And to do that, you have to have a very close bond with the person with whom you're entering that world. And so getting the right partner is absolutely critical.

An interesting side note: Hamish has travelled all over with me doing *World's Greatest Motorcycle Rides*. And not once – not *once* – has he asked, 'Can I have a go?' He owns a percentage of our company, Gladstone Motorcycles, but he's never, ever going to learn how to ride one – because motorcycling is not in Hamish's blood, business is.

He's a Land Rover Discovery man who plays golf.

Enough said.

Simpson Helmet

I've got quite a few crash helmets. But the most iconic for me is this Simpson. In fact, it's an RX2, which, obviously, was inspired by *Star Wars* and the stormtroopers.

I got it in 1980, and it was what motorcycling then was all about. Of course, it's known today as the helmet that Stig made famous on *Top Gear*, but I had it about fifteen years before him, and my one has got a black visor and it's fucking cool, man.

It's got a great big rat legal sticker on it, but needless to say, it's totally illegal on the road here.

It's also got that great big D-ring sticking out of it to hold your head in place while you're experiencing mega G-force on oval circuits, Indy racing in America, and you lock the helmet in on a bungee cord to help you with the G-force.

This, again, is a style icon. A Simpson helmet, black visor, tiny number plate, jacked rear end, full race exhaust pipe and you were the don on the road, man. All three of those were illegal – and that made it even more fun.

Chapter 32

After doing the sex guides, I got an invite to lunch with Jeff Ford, who'd just been appointed Head of Acquisitions at Channel 5.

So I was sitting there with Jeff and he said he was looking for a car show.

I said, 'I want to do this show called *Stars and Cars*.'

Jeff said, 'That sounds great. We'll do that.'

And then I added, 'Oh, and, er, I'm going to present it.'

'What?' he said. 'You can't present.'

And I said, 'Well, look. I know the stars, right, and I know the cars inside out too. So it only makes sense that I present it.'

'No, Henry, I'm not interested. If you get someone else to do it, I'll do the show.'

So we ate lunch, and I was sitting there thinking about it, and although I only made that decision over the menu, I knew I wanted to present.

After *Mad Dogs*, I didn't give a shit what happened to me. No one could throw any more shit at me than had already been thrown.

So at the end of lunch, I went, 'Jeff, look, can we just go back to *Stars and Cars* again?'

'Yeah, you're not presenting it.'

I said, 'Hang on. I'll make you a one-off special for free, right. If it rates, give me a series; if it doesn't, buy me lunch here, and I'll buy this one.'

He goes, 'Oh, fucking hell, all right, then.'

So we went and made it, and it rated. And we did a series and then we did Christmas specials for five years after that.

It changed my life. I got the strength from the disaster of *Mad Dogs* to be able to be in front of the camera.

But it got off to a bad start. The first day of shooting, I'll never forget, I had to do three pieces to camera. Total disaster. I started sweating, I forgot my words, I did another version and another, and I was sweating more and rushing it. And by the end, when we finally got it done, I was in pieces.

That night, I rang Sebastian, the war cameraman who had rescued me from Paula.

I said, 'Seb, you've worked with every presenter in the world – help me, man. I don't know who to be in front of camera.'

He asked, 'What do you mean?'

I said, 'I don't know who to be, you know? Who I'm supposed to be. How am I supposed to act. What way am I supposed to act?'

'What the fuck do you mean, Henry?' said Seb. 'Just be yourself. If the viewers don't like you being yourself, tough shit. But they definitely won't like you pretending to be someone else. The only hope you've got is to be you.'

'Oh, thanks,' I went, then put the phone down.

And from that day on, I've always been me.

Chapter 33

The point is, none of this would ever have happened if *Mad Dogs* had been a success. I'd never, ever have presented anything.

And of course, from doing shows about cars it was just a short hop back to doing shows about bikes.

Motorcycling as a spiritual way of life has been all pervading in my life.

I'd suggested *Stars and Cars* because I knew they were looking for a car show, no other reason. But all the while – my whole life, really – I was thinking, 'How am I going to get bikes on telly?'

This was the mission.

And so after *Stars and Cars* had been going on a few years I went and met with the Travel Channel. They were tiny in the UK, but big globally, and I sat down with the bloke who owned it, a guy called Richard Wolf. We came up with a series called *Great Drives of the World*, where I drove different cars in different parts of the world, and talked shit with people.

We delivered the shows, and I went to see Richard again, and he said, 'They were great. They've gone down really well, rated really well, Henry.'

I said, 'Cool, man. Now look, right, what I really want to do is a bike show. And I want to buy a Harley and ride Route 66.'

He went, 'Well, could you do me one more series of *Great Drives*?'

'All right,' I said. 'I'll do you another series of *Great Drives* if you guarantee me – in fact, you commission on the same contract – Route 66 on a Harley.'

And that trip became the first *World's Greatest Motorcycle Rides*, with me riding across America on a Heritage Softail Springer, which I bought in Chicago.

I turned up at Lakeshore Harley Davidson, the iconic Harley shop, and I said, 'I'm going to ride Route 66 now-ish, like tomorrow.'

'It's 2800 miles to LA, man.'

'Yeah, I know. So, er, what bike should I buy, then – because I don't know a thing about Harleys.'

'Dude, man, you just need that Springer, dude.'

'Er, ok. How much is that?'

'Seven and a half thousand bucks, man. We can have it ready for you by the morning.'

'Great. Here's the credit card.'

So the next morning, I got on that bike, and off I went.

Now, up to that moment I'd genuinely thought, Anyone who drives a Harley is a cunt. And I got on that bike, and I was coming out of Chicago, wondering when I was going to be converted. It was just like a tractor, I thought. The gear shift was just clunk, clunk. It was so insanely heavy, everything about it . . .

But by the time I got to Springfield (where the Simpsons come from), about 90 miles west of Chicago, I suddenly realized what Harley Davidsons are all about, which is:

America. If you're going to ride American roads, you do not want to be on anything but a Harley because it's the most incredibly comfortable motorcycle you've ever sat on.

Once it gets up to speed, you're in top gear, you are doing two and a half thousand revs, and it's going *ba, ba, ba, ba, ba, ba, ba, ba, ba, ba*, you can light a fag, you can set it to cruise control and you can mess about – because it's not going to move. It's totally predictable. You are king of the road. You've got your feet up and the bikers coming the other way give you two fingers – they're not giving you the bird, your two fingers are by your left knee – it means 'two wheels'.

And suddenly, you are part of motorcycling folklore. You're riding the American dream. You're on a great big hog, but everyone respects you for being on that hog – because they're on one too. You're part of a worldwide community. And you're on a bike that will do 95 or 100 and it'll do it all day long. And when you get off it, whether it's 100 miles or 300 miles to the next petrol station, you don't feel as though you've ridden at all. It's not like when you get off a Ducati 916 and go, 'Jesus, ah my back, my arsehole, my cock's numb'.

It's not like that. It's just this armchair.

A Harley is what riding the American dream is all about, you know. And within 90 miles of setting off, I never wanted that ride to end, which is why I've done Route 66 three times since.

Route 66 really is the story of America. People had built their lives in the 20s in the east, right. Then came the meltdown, the Depression, the Dust Bowl, Prohibition, everything. Lawlessness. For people who really had tried their hardest, and they couldn't make it work because of factors beyond their control.

Route 66 – which was first instigated in 1927 – is actually a road alignment. It was ribbons of road that were all, mostly, in existence, give or take stretches and they linked it up and called it Route 66.

Route 66 was created for the first ever motorized migration of a population west, to follow their dreams.

And then you get deeper into the history of 66: the first petrol station; the first motel; the first diner in the world; the first roadside advertising. All these things that sprang up on 66 for the first time because this had never happened to people before.

You can make a pretty decent argument that 66 was the catalyst for our pop culture today – through communication, through transportation, through leisure industries.

They call it the mother road. And for me – to ride that mother road, with everything that had happened to me in the previous five years – it meant that I connected with the shit that those first people to travel it went through.

We look at Route 66 now through rose-tinted glasses, but back then it was all about pain: the strain, the troubles, the fear that those people must have had. It's mind boggling. California? What's that?

One thing I can say for sure about 66 (at the risk of sounding like one of those drivel-talking mindfulness coaches), is that it's not about the destination, it's about the journey. And actually, if you really consider that statement, applying it to life, the drivel talkers have a good point.

Everyone is chasing their materialistic tail in this world, whether it's to get a new Vauxhall Nova on tick or whether it's to buy a tower block.

Motorcycling is here to tell you none of it makes you happy. What makes you happy is enjoying the now and enjoying the journey of life as best you can. And having come out of four years of utter shit, Route 66 seemed to clarify that for me.

I didn't really want to get to LA, thanks, anyway. I really just want to be here, on the road, or in this little motel, where it's safe.

1957 Vietnam Army Truck

This guy is a monster, a total bastard.

I have it parked out on the lawn. There's a footpath that runs past us, and the other day this dogwalker shouted out, 'What the hell is that, Henry? Jesus Christ, are you invading Oxfordshire?'

Well, as I told him, what it is is a 1957 American army truck from the Vietnam war. It's multifuel, with a 6.2-litre engine. This particular truck was originally a tipper, but it was obviously modified to be a sort of cargo or troop carrier.

I love vehicles that capture a moment in history – vehicles that are just so iconic and imbued to their very core with a particular time.

And what I mean by that is, you look at this truck and you just go, 'Vietnam'.

If you get up into the cab, and look at the dials and all that kind of stuff, you can easily imagine you are getting your ass shot off in Vietnam. Can you imagine? You could go through a house with it (and they probably did).

It's a transportation vehicle for a killing machine, a war vehicle. Like most people who have seen it first hand, I hate war, and I am not into militarism. But I have certain military vehicles because they are an art form in themselves in their devotion to purpose.

One detail I love is the red guidance balls on the rods coming up from the bumper because they tell you exactly how wide you are and where your bumper is – because when you're riding up there, it's quite difficult to see either of those situations.

When you fire it up, holy smoke – it's just fantastic. Even though everything about it is brutal and purposeful, rather than aesthetically driven, it is actually a thing of beauty.

I love being the curator of that Mack. It will outlive me. Some other nutbar will buy it off me and go off and run it.

Chapter 34

Since that first trip on Route 66, I've done the Deep South, the Wild West, the deserts of America and California Highway 1 and they have all been amazing in their own ways. In total, I've done seventeen rides in America, with more to come.

I thought I'd never be able to get enough of riding motorcycles in America. But then I did Boston to Key West, and it was a huge disappointment – and once again, the root cause was Hamish and I trusting too much in looking at maps while sitting in the office.

I knew we would be riding through some urban areas, but I just had this vision of getting out into the Carolinas and hitting Miami hard, South Beach on a chop, immersing myself yet again in the American dream.

Well, let me tell you, the east coast of America from Boston down to North Carolina ain't the American dream.

It's a fucking nightmare.

I bought a Saxon Crown with a rigid rear end and a saddle half-an-inch thick with no springs. I mean, it had no rear suspension and front forks made of monkey metal.

Now, it looked incredible, this sled – it was the coolest, most minimal chopper you could possibly ever imagine: an old-school, raked-out bobber.

So we set out from Boston on our 4000-mile odyssey and it was all going all right until I started to get a misfire off the S&S motor; when you opened the throttle, it went *ba, ba, ba, ba, ba, baa*, and then carried on, and however much I twiddled and fiddled with it, I couldn't clear it.

I went to three Harley dealers on the way down, but that misfire wasn't actually cured until I got to Miami, by which time I only had 300 miles left down to Key West. (It was an electrical fault that we couldn't find; Eddie Trotta, the legendary chop builder in Miami found it almost immediately.)

Anyway, there I was, leaving Boston with a bit of a misfire on this chopper with no front mudguard, when the rain bucketed down (we were catching the tail end of a tropical storm that was coming up from the Gulf of Mexico). So I had a constant plume of water hitting me in the face, and that's ok, if you're just doing some bar hopping on a bike. But when you're doing 4000 miles, it's not ok.

So I'm riding along, bent double to my right or to my left, so that the plume of water will go past my ear. And that's bad enough, but the other thing with this chop was that it also had almost no rear mudguard either. So I had another plume of water going up my back and over my head.

I'd always thought it would be cool to ride into New York on a crazy chopper. But, if it's raining torrentially, you're coming in through the Bronx in rush hour, at night, trying to avoid the New York potholes which are famous because they are so big there are people living in them – well, that's not cool.

(Also, don't ride a motorbike into New York unless you plan on leaving the same day because you can't park it. All the parking in Manhattan is valet, but the valet parkers can't ride motorbikes, so they don't want you in their car parks. And you can't park the bike on the street because it'll get towed away or nicked within twenty minutes. So you have to bung the valet parkers fifty bucks to park your bike, and then you have to ride it in there and park it up.)

Anyway, it turned out New York was just the start of the nightmare. We went down through Philadelphia, Baltimore, Washington, D.C. – and the urban sprawl never ended. Two thousand miles of traffic lights.

Where was the American dream now? Well, people have built over it. So if anyone ever says to you, 'Let's go down the east coast of America!' tell them to fuck off. Because they've obviously never been there. If you want a superficially glamorous North Circular that is never-ending, ride the east coast of America down to North Carolina.

The thing about being on a bike – and this is both a good thing and a bad thing – is that any place you go, you don't see what the usual crap tourists see (which, in the case of Miami, for example, is superficial bubble-gum art-deco shit). On a bike, you actually see the real place; you see and smell a very different world from what other tourists see.

I've done great drives in cars and you don't really meet anyone. It's not just because you're physically in that tin-can bubble – I mean, it's not as if you are chatting to people while you are on the bike either, but cars just physically remove you so much from your environment. Half the time, in a car, you don't even know how warm or cold it is, and that separateness seeps into your mentality.

When you're on a motorcycle, you're open to the elements – and not only the natural elements, but also the elements of society that you ride through.

If you pull up on a bike, you've got nowhere to hide if someone comes over and goes, 'Howdy'. You've got to talk to them and, nine times out of ten, it's a great experience. And also, you have the community of riders. A worldwide community is there for you as a motorcyclist. You are part of a club, and if you do break down, someone is going to stop for you. (And you should do the same and stop for them, you know, unless they're on a GS.)

So no disrespect to anyone who lives in Miami, I just don't like the place. It smacks of commercialism and I got the vibe that people want to take what they can from you. I hated the commercialism of South Beach and I couldn't wait to leave there on the bike.

There was a pot of gold at the end of the rainbow, however, and that was the 320-mile ride to Key West over incredible bridges down the keys. They are fabulous roads and make for a truly amazing, mind-blowing ride. And then Key West itself is absolutely beautiful. It's very laid back, and the people are non-judgmental. My advice would be to go to Miami, ride through it quick and head down to Key West, but then perhaps ride east to west through the Deep South.

That first trip on Route 66 was a total and complete life changer, and the fact that the road was built to give desperate people a second chance – a chance to make success out of the failure that was going on around them – wasn't lost on me.

That is why they call it the Boulevard of Dreams.

And this Harley Davidson, it was doing that for me. It was changing my life.

It was just a little nothing to other people; they'd say, 'The Travel Channel, what's that?'

But to me, it was everything.

Chapter 35

I took any work I could to keep the cash coming in, and it was one of these jobs that led me to my closest near-death experience.

Bikers think about death more than other people for obvious reasons. I have a feeling it ain't going to be much fun, because there've been two or three times in my life where I thought I was going to die, and they weren't exactly good times.

But the very closest I came to dying, I wasn't on a bike or on drugs.

I was doing an underwater documentary in the South China Sea for BBC Classic Adventure.

I run out of talent pretty quickly underwater – I mean, I can literally hardly swim – but, for some reason I'd got myself a job as an underwater TV producer.

Sebastian rang me one Monday and he went, 'Mate, what are you doing?'

'Seb, all right, mate. Trying to run a business, I guess.'

He said, 'Look, I'm cave diving in the Bahamas, right, and I've let go of a camera and it's gone up a crevasse, and I can't get it. It's 150 feet under water in a cave. Get me another one out here, can you?'

'How am I going to do that?'

'You're on the 2:45 to Miami. I've booked your ticket already.'

So I flew out and I got picked up by a private plane and taken to South Andros, where they were filming these massive marine sinkholes – deep blue holes in the seabed with their own ecosystem – for a documentary about the Lucayan Indians who were the indigenous population of the Bahamas until they got wiped out by diseases imported by Columbus and his crew.

No one had ever found a complete skeleton of a Lucayan Indian (they'd found skulls) until Rob Palmer, a marine biologist, was diving in the blue holes and found a ledge about 150 feet down with a whole pile of Lucayan Indian skeletons. It turned out that when a Lucayan Indian died, they got lobbed in the blue holes, and that's why no one had ever found them. And also, they lobbed their live wife and livestock in with them.

So that was the story that they were doing.

Anyway, I met up with Seb and he went, 'You've dived before, have you?'

'No,' I told him.

'Well put some fucking gear on.'

I did as he said.

'Ok, jump in this pool. Can you breathe?'

'Yeah.'

'Right, you're trained. Let's go.'

And he threw me into a blue hole, first dive.

I was there for a week and I started diving with them and loved it. So when I got back home I got a diving qual-ification, and we started doing loads of underwater stuff. I filmed some of it because I was a cameraman anyway, and I knew how to operate the gear.

And that's how I ended up nearly dying in the South China Sea doing this show for BBC Classic Adventure.

The gig was, we were going to lie two white ensigns on the bows of HMS *Repulse* and HMS *Prince of Wales*, both of which were sent by Churchill to give the Japs a little bit of a hard time in World War II, but actually got sunk within four days of being in enemy waters, with the loss of 1500 lives on each boat.

We flew in to Singapore – me and Seb and a few others – and we went to get our boat down at the harbour and it was basically a cut and shut. To say it was dodgy is putting it mildly, but off we went, and about 5 miles out of Singapore harbour, on this three-week trip, the air conditioning broke and the cook got sea sick.

We were going to be hot and hungry.

Anyway, we got to the dive site and these wrecks were lying at 200 feet. No one had told us that. They'd said they were at 98 feet. Eventually, after about three days, we finally got attached to the wrecks and started diving.

It was a disaster from the start. There was a guy on the crew called Alan, who claimed he had been in the SAS, but it turned out he was the cook for them when they were on exercise in Hereford. He did not have a clue. We were doing a night dive and I just remember seeing this geezer go past me, totally out of control, going back up to the surface with only one flipper. How he'd lost the other one, I've no idea.

Then Seb woke up one morning and had a rant about something, got up on deck and ran around like he often did, shouting and screaming at everybody. Only this time, he tripped up, went head first down the deck hole, smashed his head on a load of oxygen cylinders and passed out. He came round pretty quick and coughed and spluttered and then ranted some more and we all laughed about it.

But the doctor said we had to get him off.

And the problem was, we were miles out of range of the Malaysian rescue services. So we cut all the ropes holding us onto the wreck, and steamed for three days, so we could get in range for the helicopter. They were just radioing the helicopter when the doctor said, 'Actually, he's all right.'

By the time we finally got back to the wrecks and got reattached, we were massively behind and working long days to try to catch up.

One evening, one of the other cameramen, Rob, said to me, 'I'm doing a book on plankton, Henry. Do you want to hop in and go for a night dive, just an evening dive, and help me just film some plankton, stillness and that?'

I went, 'Sure, mate, that'll be fun.'

So, I togged up, the dive master ticked us off and Rob and I jumped in.

The dive master went off for a beer, Rob went down and then I started to try to go down too. Only, I couldn't. Seb had nicked three weights off my weight belt and I hadn't checked it, so I couldn't go down. And on the surface, the current was running really strong, way stronger than 50 feet down, so I was drifting off.

And drifting off fast.

The swell was six feet and it was getting dark.

The dive master was round the other side of the boat with his beer, so no one could hear or see me. Stupidly, I tried to swim against the current to get back to the boat, and within about two minutes I was totally knackered and moving away from the boat really, really fast.

That was the one moment where I genuinely thought I was going to die. It was actually quite peaceful because I'd given up. I thought, Well that's it. I'm just going to bob off now and that's the end. I hope Janie finds someone nice to take my place. Then, suddenly, Rob popped up next to me.

Was I glad to see that guy! He coupled himself onto me, but we kept floating away. We were virtually out of range when the dive master walked round from the other side and saw us.

I could not even pull myself onto the little rubber rescue dinghy when it arrived. They had to haul me in.

You know that old saying, that no one here gets out alive? It's true, man. And as you get older, you realize the futility of life. But rather than that being depressing, it is immensely liberating. In fact, the sooner you get how futile life is, the sooner you can truly enjoy it.

I heard about a study the other day that said you are at your happiest over the age of forty-seven. That's definitely been true for me. In my twenties and thirties, I thought I was going to be Jonathan Ross or Franco Zeffirelli.

I'm never going to be either of those and it took me until my late forties to realize that at a gut level. But then I was able to stop trying and accept that much as I thought, at the age of twenty-five or thirty-two, that I was going to have my own chat show on BBC1, we are sorry to inform you, Henry, that ain't going to happen. And, by the way, your first movie proved you are a talentless movie director, so, if for one moment you think you might get a second chance, you're mistaken.

What that does to you is make you humble. It also makes you realize that, actually, life's ok. And I may not be Zeffirelli or Jonathan Ross, but I've probably got twenty brilliant years ahead of me in which I don't have to worry about that shit any more.

And consequently, I can say, 'I'll do what I want to do from now on'. Because when I'm lying there on my deathbed (if I'm lucky enough to realize that I am on it), and I say to myself, 'Have you got any regrets, son?' I can reply in the negative.

I'd be incredibly arrogant to believe it makes any difference whatsoever whether Henry Cole is alive or dead because it means nothing. But that doesn't mean I don't want to be alive, feeling ok on a day like today.

That's what failure, near-death experiences and motorcycling do for you.

1954 Austin Healey 100/4

For a car to play a part in my life it's got to represent bare-bones motoring, whether it's a Land Rover Series 3, a Willys Jeep or this, my Austin Healey.

The Austin Healey is one of the most iconic British sports cars of all time, along with Aston Martin, the E-Type and the XK Jaguar. It just so happened that my mate Angus had this car for sale and I would never, ever have thought really of buying an Austin Healey, but this one to me is special because it's the 1954 Earl's Court car and it was bought by a geezer who kept it till 2011. He spent seventy-five thousand quid restoring it – then he died in 2013. The car is rally-spec with 100-M engine in it. It was called the 100/4 because it did a hundred miles an hour on four cylinders.

So I came across this car at Angus's and I am actually the second owner from new, which is quite incredible. It is unmarked, in mint, concourse condition.

Britain was finally coming out of the shadow of the war when this was built in 1954, and there was great expectation that we would lead the way in the engineering of motorcycles and cars. It was an icon of hope.

I don't really like anyone seeing me in it. I know that sounds weird, but I didn't buy it to pose in. I bought it because it's a car I love for its aesthetics and its performance. I usually drive it on a Sunday morning really early doors, when there's no one around and the roads are empty. And that's when it comes into its own. It handles beautifully. For my money it's one of the prettiest cars ever to be made.

What I also find fascinating about these old cars is that safety was really not at the forefront of anyone's mind back then, and as cars have got safer they have got duller. Design and performance were prevalent, and for us, making motorcycles, that's still the same today. Bikes ain't ever gonna be safe, so that frees us up to make them look as amazing as possible.

Honestly, if I'm on my own or with mates, I don't give two fucks about vehicle safety. All I'm interested in is being part of a motoring icon, by riding or driving one. And the element of danger in this car – that it's basically going to concertina on you if you hit anything – won't stop me driving it. I am not going to be putting an airbag in it any time soon. I've got racing seat belts in it, but, to be honest, that won't stop the engine ending up on my lap.

It's the same with all these old cars: if I have an accident, it's not going to go well. But saying that, a mate of mine recently rolled a Willys Jeep and got out to tell the tale. How that happened, fuck knows, but he's only about two foot tall now.

Chapter 36

Weirdly, I am sort of famous now, to the people that matter, that is, and I never get bored of talking to fans.

It started to happen with *World's Greatest Motorcycle Rides*. The very first time, I was in Helsinki getting on a plane. Three ladies came up to me and wanted to hug me and take a photo. And I left that situation thinking, Do they honestly know who I am? Or do they think I am Charley Boorman? (I was often mistaken for him in the early days, to the point where people would come up and go: 'Mate!' I'd say, 'I'm not Charley Boorman.' And they'd say, 'Aren't you?' And walk off.)

One really memorable time I was recognized was in the Deep South. I was standing outside, having a fag, and this American lawyer came out and randomly went, 'I've just been watching this British guy rant about America and shit on a motorbike . . . holy shit, that's you!'

When I go to a bike show, it's mayhem, and I love it. It takes me half an hour to go for a piss. Five years, ten years later, and I still can't quite believe people want to talk to me.

And the point is, I want to talk to them.

People have come up to me and said, 'Henry, I saw your show and I've just ridden Route 66.'

Great chat.

Or, 'Mate, I saw your show. Sam showed me how to do this Triumph, so I bought one; look man.'

And out comes the phone.

I have so much to chat to those people about. And that's the thing about the notoreity I have today: it's got nothing to do with restaurants and film premieres – it's just about a shared passion.

I go to the NEC bike show in Birmingham and I get mobbed – and it's the most fantastic experience. A global community comes to Birmingham once a year to look at motorcycles and talk shit, and that makes me feel part of life.

Or I go to the Newark Autojumble, right (which is Birmingham for people with no teeth), and I'm with kindred spirits.

It's uplifting; I'm part of a tribe.

Chapter 37

I really hope that I never become a smug bastard. One thing I hate is smug bastards. They normally come from the middle class, of which I am undeniably a member, but I still feel, like every other biker I have ever met, that I was born to be a rebel.

In a sense, I have my father to thank for that. Whatever his faults as a modern parent, he sure did bring me up to be an individual.

For example, I don't have much time for one of the biggest causes of the smugocracy: electric cars.

We, as a country, produce precisely 1.21 per cent of the world's emissions, so it genuinely does not matter whether I'm driving a V12, a Prius or a half-hearted attempt at a hybrid – you know, one of those motors that just happens to have a petrol engine in case you run out of juice. Until China and America even accept that there is global warming, it's all nonsense.

But the smug bastards pretend not to know that. Drive a motorbike or a fast car or, God forbid, an *old* car and you are a mass murderer and an idiot.

But the smug bastards get to dominate the debate. They dictate the rules because they have not only got time on their hands and money, they also, unfortunately, have some intelligence and expensive educations and totally right-on buzzwords, which make them sound very convincing.

And we sit here, the silent majority who know it's bollocks, doing nothing because the quinoa-eating smug bastards have monopolized the conversation, and they are taking advantage of the fact that we can't be arsed to have an argument with them because all we want to do in life is get a job, have a couple of sprogs and go out for a spin on the bike.

I am not a political animal. Politicians are nearly all self-serving wankers in my opinion.

They spin everything. They lie to us. And the joke's on us because we elect them into a nice little earner, a lovely little restaurant allowance, a great pad in London and all that caper. And then, even if they start out by trying to make a difference, politicians quickly become quinoa people.

I could easily have become a quinoa person. I know I'm privileged. I make TV shows. But I also go out and I hang out with people in sheds and nutbars on bikes and I know those people hate the fact that they're not being heard.

The pinnacle of smugness right now, in my opinion, is the anti-vaping movement.

Attacks on vaping are everywhere. Why can't I vape in a hotel room? It doesn't smell.

But there's the sign: No Vaping.

Fuck you, man! It makes me want to throw the telly out the window, trash the gaff and then blow vape smoke at them as I'm leaving.

And a new law, specially designed by the smug bastards, says that you can't buy vape juice in anything larger than 10ml bottles. A European law, right, because little Klaus drank a bottle of vape juice.

So what happens? I buy ten 10ml bottles, pour them into one big bottle and now I have ten plastic bottles to chuck away, which, hopefully, won't be swallowed by a seal that's minding its own business trying to have a few sprogs and paddle about.

The vape police are typical of how the smug bastards have zero concept of life on the ground. Vaping is the most incredible thing to happen to public health in a century. I was a hardcore smoker: forty a day, for forty years. I smoked regularly from the age of thirteen and it was almost certainly going to cost the NHS a lot of money and eventually kill me.

Then I switched to vaping. I go for a mixture with 3mg nicotine. It's got a little hint of menthol and aniseed going on, costs sixty-four quid for 100ml and that will last me a month.

On the fags, I was smoking two packs a day, so that was about a hundred and forty quid a week at the end. And I smoked like that for thirty years.

I switched to vaping a few years back because I couldn't be arsed to go downstairs from a hotel room one night. Haven't had a fag since. Me – who did nothing else apart from smoke after I gave up the heroin and the drink. I'll be three years clean of fags soon.

Vaping has changed my life.

Completely.

I look about ten years younger for starters.

People say, 'Oh well, the long-term effects are unknown . . .' But do they honestly think I give a monkey's? A man who did two hundred and fifty quid's worth of heroin, a load of freebase coke *and* forty Silk Cut a day – am I supposed to be concerned that vaping might harm me?

Do I give a nicotine-smoked sausage?

No. I do not.

All I know is that my doctor says to me, 'How are you getting on, Henry? You're looking all right.'

And I go, 'Well, I'm vaping.'

And he goes, 'Keep vaping.'

Vaping has transformed life for millions of people. Whoever invented it should be given a knighthood because it's saving the NHS billions of pounds. But they won't get one because it's only chavs who vape and smoke, and we are not on the smug bastards' radar.

And the people who make all the accusations about vaping, the people who want to ban it because their little children might try it – they just don't have a clue.

They are smug bastardry personified.

Series 3 Land Rover

If you have a soft spot for any British vehicle, it has to be a Land Rover. I've got two of them. Mine have this funny effect on people; when you're driving along, people wave at you.

My most-loved vehicles either sum up a period of time or an atmosphere, and the Land Rover does both.

We have a duty to look after these things. They're part of our history, just as much as King Alfred and Henry VIII. A Land Rover is something that must be treated with the respect that it deserves.

Whenever I give someone a ride in mine, they always tell me about childhood memories of going in one. You could spend two hundred and fifty grand on a Lamborghini, but you'll never get that reaction.

They stopped making Defenders because they were not Euro compliant. But people love them so much that now they're buying up all the old Range Rovers and series Land Rovers and doing a classic programme at Land Rover.

So you can buy a two-door Range Rover now for a hundred and sixty grand, completely specced out by Land Rover.

Apparently, they are having trouble getting their hands on the old vehicles because they have to buy them off shed dwellers, and they ask for an invoice and pay later.

You're dealing with a geezer in a shed. It's cash money right now, son. And if it ain't, you ain't having it.

Chapter 38

I got to have a second pop at my music career in 2010.

I was making a show called *Men Brewing Badly* with Neil Morrissey. The idea was that Neil, who has a microbrewery, was going to drive all this beer that he'd made down to the World Cup, through Africa, to give to the England fans, while we won the World Cup.

It was clearly a terrible idea – and I'd like to point out I didn't think it up – but the good thing that came out of it was that I met Neil and became friends with him, and there couldn't be a nicer dude on the planet. What a top geezer he is.

Anyway, we had to do a title track for the show, and I thought, I've always wanted to do rock and roll; this is my big chance.

So I got Neil to front this track with me on the drums, to the tune of 'In the Jungle' – but instead of, 'the lion sleeps tonight', it was 'three lions score tonight'. We had a complete ball with this track, so I released it on the record label that I quickly conceived. It cost me in total about ten grand to do it and I got seven grand back at the end of the day.

We actually got to number 77 in the charts. We played on *Good Morning Britain* and we were going to do Glastonbury and the Wire Festival – we were booked to go on and give it rock all in between sets on the main stage. But obviously England were shit and got knocked out, so we were cancelled. We should have released the track in 2018!

Still, it was a dream fulfilled for me; and if you fulfil your dreams, however small, then you can die happy.

Chapter 39

I'm chronically uncompetitive.

I have the best time of my life every time it's a beautiful sunny day and I'm riding and I really don't give a shit whether someone passes me or not. I ride a bike for deeper reasons than coming third in some race at Oulton Park. I think that's why I'd never raced a motorcycle, until I attempted the land speed record at the Bonneville Salt Flats, which was, to be honest, quite a way to start.

I got a call from Mark Upham, who owns Brough Superior, asking me if I'd be interested in trying to set a new land speed record on one of their vintage bikes.

Mark's everything that I love about a human being, mainly because he does not give a monkey's about what anyone else thinks of him. He's a totally eccentric aristocrat who lives in Austria. He'd always had a thing about Brough Superiors, so when he got a chance to buy the brand, he did.

Mark knew that Brough Superior had a long history of sprinting and land speed attempts back in the day, and he wanted to get back that part of the brand's heritage.

His idea was to go and break six land speed records at the Bonneville Salt Flats, so he rang me and he went, 'Dear boy, I wonder whether you'd care to involve yourself in attempting a land speed record?'

And I went, 'Mark, you're talking to me. Of course I wouldn't. Because I'd just be fucking terrified.'

Anyway, Mark's just not the kind of guy you can say no to, so I ended up agreeing to do it. There are different categories at Bonneville, and my target was one of the vintage classes; basically, this meant that I was going to be riding a 1927 Brough Superior motorcycle – complete with 1927 technology.

Mark put together a team of three of us to attempt the six records. The other two riders were Alan 'Crashcart' Cathcart, who is one of the greatest motorcycle reviewers and writers ever, and Eric Patterson, who was seventy-two, and I don't think he would mind me saying he is a loon-head speed freak who is wired up to the wrong Mars bar. People say you're going to be going slower as you get older, but try telling Eric that.

So I said to Mark, 'Ok, so, what's it like, riding on the salt, then?'

He went, 'Well, dear boy, it's a bit of an issue.'

And I said, 'Go on, then.'

'Well,' he started, 'firstly it's like riding on ice. So you'll have no front brake at all. We just don't put a front brake on it.'

And I went, 'What do you mean by that, Mark?'

He went, 'Well, if you have an issue, you'll naturally pull the front brake, because that's what bikers do. Problem is, the minute you do that on the salt, you're off. So it's much easier just . . . not to put one on.'

'So you're asking me to ride a 1927 motorcycle at speeds of what, a hundred, a hundred and ten miles an hour with no front brake on a surface akin to ice?'

'That's right. The only thing you really have to worry about is if something blows up. Or you get a shimmy.'

'What's a shimmy?'

'Well, it's like a tank slapper.'

A tank slapper is a horrible thing where the front wheel of the bike starts to shake. You can't control it. It just gets worse and worse until, in the end, it's like riding a bucking horse.

'Mark, the only way you can ditch a tank slapper on a road is to drop a gear, open her up and then hope the acceleration will clear you through it. But if you're on ice, and you drop a gear at a hundred, the back wheel will spin out and you're toast.'

'Yes, dear boy. All you've got to do is fucking hang on.'

'Christ, you're not half flattering me, Mark.'

I spent a year training for Bonneville, in the course of which I broke my shoulder when I came off on a dirt-bike track, and for some time it looked like I wasn't going to be able to go.

But several months of (agonizing) physiotherapy got me back on two wheels. Thank God. I don't know what I would have done if I couldn't ride a bike again.

After all the chat about ice, the first thing I wanted to do when I finally got to Bonneville was go and look at the surface.

The Bonneville Salt Flats were formed through the evaporation of a massive prehistoric lake in Utah. It's just this extraordinary expanse of hard white salt crust, totally flat. It's as big as the lake was: about 12 miles long and 5 miles wide.

The surface is, for the most part, really hard, especially on the tracks – called the straightways – because they compact it by dragging great big railway sleepers behind trucks.

The darker the salt is, the harder it is. You want to avoid any white patches, because that's where it's fluffy and the front wheel could dig in.

They've got two straightways next to each other: if you're doing sub-150mph, which I was, you're on the mountain straight. That's a 2-mile run-up, 1-mile Flying Mile and a 2-mile run-down. The second is the international straight, which is 11 miles long with a 5-mile run-up and a 5-mile run-down, and that straight is for legends doing up to 400mph. The most dangerous part is the run-down. That's where most people come off. They go through the Flying Mile, say, 'I've done it', then shut off the throttle real quick and the whole bike goes out of shape.

What you want to do instead is what the veterans call 'the long, slow squeeze'. It's a style of riding that is very alien. But basically, everything that you do at Bonneville should be done very, very slow – apart from what you're actually doing, of course. You can always tell who the rookies are because the flag goes down and then you can hear them, giving it some serious wellie. It's like, 'Fucking hell, mate, you've got two fucking miles; what are you doing?'

The weirdest thing about Bonneville is that you're not racing against somebody else, where they're all round you and you're tucked in on the bend and you pull out and there's another cunt and you've got to knee him out of the way. There's nothing like that. You're on your own. You are racing against history, not people, and that's why a lot of track racers hate it, because you get yourself prepared and you've got a lot of things to think about.

But in that Flying Mile, you're lying on this fucking bike. You're lying on it, it's 1927, right, and it should be only doing 40. And you're just waiting for it to go bang. And you've got your fingers on the clutch like you're waiting, you know. And then you go through the Flying Mile, you go through the timing thing and then you run down slowly, slowly, slowly. Then you have to come back to impound – I can't remember what it's called, come back to stage, pre-stage, you know. And get your timing chit. If it says you are close or pass or beating that record or you set a decent record time, you're then allowed to go back and run again – because you've got to do it both ways, to get your average speed, in case you have a steaming great tail wind.

Bonneville started in the 1920s with the 11-mile straight – a 5-mile run up, 1-mile Flying, 5-mile run-down. There isn't anywhere else in the world that can offer an 11-mile straight that's flat and where nothing's going to run out at you.

Bonneville is 6500 feet above sea level. It is the most incredibly difficult environment to ride a motorcycle in. If you are normally aspirated – not turbo or fuel-injection because that isn't really affected by altitude – and you are doing 150 here testing, you're probably going to average 120 at Bonneville, because of the altitude and hostility of the environment.

It changes rapidly as well. You can run a test at Bonneville at four in the afternoon, and that run is beautiful. You've jetted it right; you've sorted it all out. Then, you run at seven in the morning when you're going for it, and the fucking thing won't work because the atmosphere has changed. It's very damp in the mornings at Bonneville. And as it dries out, the bikes run leaner, right. So you've got to get it absolutely cock on, you know, to go for it. Doing Bonneville was the most incredible experience, not least because that's how I met Sam Lovegrove, my co-presenter on *Shed and Buried*, *Find It, Fix It, Drive It*, and a new show called *Junk and Disorderly*. It was Sam who built the Brough Superior that I rode to land speed record success at Bonneville.

The man's a legend.

Sam Lovegrove is a very dark horse. For example, what you might not realize from watching him arse about with me in the van is that he is a genius. I mean, really. He was chief of design and development at a company where, from 1998 to 2001, he ran a team of thirty people designing hydrogen fuel cells that would eventually power taxis and buses.

He flew all around the world doing this, designing cutting-edge technology, but then he did what we all dream of doing but haven't got the balls to do: he chucked in the hundred-grand-a-year job to follow his passion, which is pre-war cars and motorcycles.

He is, without question, the world leader on Brough Superior restoration. People give him responsibility for their

£100,000–500,000 motorcycles. Jay Leno relies on him for his restos.

At the moment, he's got a very wealthy client who sent him a frame and half a Brough SS100 engine. Sam has recreated and milled out the other half of the engine.

He's made the other half of the engine. The cases, everything. And you can't tell what's the new bit and what's the old one. That's genius.

He was the instigator or the creator of one of the most incredible moments of my life, which was doing that land speed record. And sharing with somebody the pain, the anguish, the self-doubt that you have when you're lying on a bike before you launch it at Bonneville is a great starter to a relationship. We just got on so well on the salt, and shared so many interests, that we immediately bonded.

To be honest, it's very difficult at my age to make new friends – proper ones. Most of my friends are from school or from motorcycling in the early days. So to find someone who was so like-minded in one way, but so completely not like-minded in others (you know, the guy's a bean-eating hippy and I'm as far away from that as you can possibly be) was amazing and our relationship burgeoned.

I knew Sam would be great on telly, so I went to him with the idea of *Shed and Buried* and said, 'This is what I want to do, this is how I want to do it. Why don't we just give it a run?'

And therein lies another part of his character. Because most people who live in sheds and restore really expensive top-end motorcycles will stay in their shed and do just that.

But he took the risk and said, 'All right. We'll give it a go, see what happens.'

And so he's come with me on this journey over the last six years. We spend our days rummaging around other people's sheds and restoring stuff in ours. You can't get better than that. And that's called *work*, by the way.

There've been relationships in my life that I've wanted to continue and ended up not doing it for different reasons. But you only meet a certain number of these people in your life, and when you do, you must try everything in your power to hang on to them. And thank God I did that with Sam. I really gave it a proper go and he's become one of my dearest mates.

The reason why we work together on camera is purely down to the fact that our friendship is genuine. We don't give a fuck what we say on telly. We don't give a fuck that the camera's rolling. If we open a shed and there's a shitter in there, we will say so. If we open the shed and there's a Norton Inter in the corner, we will both go mad, you know. We also know that whatever we say to each other is for love rather than one-upmanship. There is no ego between the two of us. We are much more interested in the subject matter than in our own positions on that subject matter. So I don't give a fuck whether Sammy's doing an interview or I'm doing it, if he's riding the bike or I'm riding it. And neither does he. It never even crosses our minds.

There are other people out there who have a relationship like we do – the Hairy Bikers, for example. You can tell with those two lads that they're for real. And if a relationship is an honest one, and if it can be seen by people to be quite humorous or endearing, then you've got yourself a hit show.

But you can't organize that. You can't, as an exec producer, make that happen. It's got to come from the heart. And everything that Sammy and I do really does come from the heart. And that's why we're doing so much now for Channel 4, ITV1 and ITV4 together – because it is a genuine relationship.

We're aspirational in a non-aspirational way, by which I mean we're not flying off to the Luxor in Vegas and snorting coke – we're just in a shed, man. Because that's where we want to be and that's what we love. It's accessible and it's attainable and it's where we want to be.

Anyway, back to Bonneville.

The record we're going for is pre-1955, 750, push rod, normally aspirated, running on gas rather than dope methanol.

To qualify, the engine cases and the barrels have to be original 20s, pre-55. The rest of it you have to do in the style of it, absolutely how it is, but a lot of it can be new. Because otherwise you're going to die. Using 1927 forks isn't a good idea.

We test the Brough for about a year.

I'm just a road rider, and I've never ridden a motorcycle for the be all and end all to be speed. Speed is part of it, but certainly not all of it for me. There's always someone who's got more talent than me.

Now, I'm riding this bike purely for speed, and I think that will put all the emotional and philosophical reasons as to why I ride a motorcycle into the background.

In fact, it is the complete reverse.

The morning of the run arrives. I've been asking some of the greatest racers in the world for their advice. And they tell me – you won't believe this – they tell me to lay my head sideways on the tank, looking at what in normal circumstances would be the hedge. The theory is that it is more aerodynamic, and you're not going to hit anything and you can see where you are by the distance between you and the markers.

Yeah, right.

So I ride up to the start. You have to queue for about five hours – in your full leathers, in 40-degree heat. You wait and you wait and then you wait.

Then someone's GoPro falls off, and they've got to find that. They have to search 5 miles of salt. They've got to find that bit of shit before anyone else can run.

Eventually, I get to the start, with Sammy by my side, of course.

I'm genuinely shitting myself now, really, because it's the unknown. I don't know what's going to happen, but I do know I could die. I could come off and kill myself. I could run out of talent pretty early on, you know, or I could get over 80mph and be happy.

So I'm lying on this bike in the boiling hot weather with Sam and a couple of other mechanics around.

And I say to Sammy, 'Give me some fucking advice, Sammy.'

And he goes, 'Just imagine you're going to the shops to get some Jaffa Cakes.'

'What the fuck do you mean by that?'

He says, 'Just go and do what you want to do. Do it how you want to do it.' And then he ties this little toy to the bike with wire.

'What are you doing that for?'

'That's my son Gregory's little toy. He said he wanted it to go down Bonneville Salt Flats.'

'Oh, all right.'

Then this dude is standing beside me with a massive green flag.

I can't see the circuit; it's just heat haze. I can't see the markers.

I'm panicking. 'Sam, I can't fucking see anything.'

Sam goes, 'Henry, you see that flat bit of the mountain, just head for that.'

Then green-flag guy says, 'You ready?'

'No. Yes.'

Then he says, 'God speed.'

He waves the flag and I'm gone.

I'm lucky that the minute I start anything, the nerves go. I don't hear anything; even the howl of the engine is kind of filtered out.

I've got points on my rev counter, but no speedo. I'm watching the rev counter, absolutely meticulously, because Sam has told me to keep it at 4600, so I don't do 4650, I do 4600 revs. I start going through the gears.

And I'm a mile out from the Flying Mile, lying on this bike, and I suddenly realize that everything that everyone told me was the reason not to do this is every single reason that I'm fucking loving every second of this shit.

I can see the Flying Mile flag coming, the start, so I get it just how Sam's told me to get it and I go into fifth and I'm in the Flying Mile. And I'm lying on this thing, like lying on it, you know. I'm gripping it with my knees and just trying to get as low as I can.

About a quarter way into the Flying Mile, I have completely forgotten any advice that anyone has given me. All I'm looking for are ruts, and I've got my two fingers on the clutch, waiting. I'm looking at where the ambulances are and all that kind of stuff. They're fucking miles away. Anyway, I'm settling in.

About three-quarters of the way down the Flying Mile, I hit a rut and nothing happens, immediately. But then, a few seconds later, it starts to go. A tank slapper starting. It gets worse and worse and worse, to the point where I can hardly hold the thing, right.

And I've still got time to think, What the fuck am I going to do here? And I'm shouting in my helmet, 'I ain't going to drop this bike. You're fucking staying upright, you cunt.'

(I later found out that that happened at 116 miles an hour.)

And I'm shouting this. It's tempting to drop a gear, but that will be a horrible wipeout. Bonneville has made the decision for me; I'm just going to hang on.

I start decreasing the speed incrementally. And by the time

I've gone through the timing light at the end of the mile, I've got control of it. I stay upright and it's cool.

There's no way you can gauge your speed, so when they come running over with the chit and it's 115 miles an hour, everyone thinks that's amazing.

Then we have to do it the other way.

Alan Cathcart is up at the other end.

He says, 'Mate, just do exactly what you did before. You're setting a record, you know, so just enjoy the return run. You can do it.'

So God speed, off I go.

And I'm changing up into second, third and it starts to misfire.

I should stop, but I take a decision: fuck it. I'm doing this.

And actually, as I am making that decision, she starts to clear a bit, so I just lie on her and go. She misfires quite substantially on the return, and I only do 95 miles an hour or something.

But I get the record.

And on one level, that was it. We packed up and went home. But what was really amazing about it all was finding Sam. *Shed and Buried* started there, with our relationship. You meet very few people who you trust with your life. I faced my ultimate fear with Sam and he guided me through that.

But the most incredible thing of all is that on the day of breaking that record, I was twenty-five years clean. To the day. I got clean on 26 August 1988 and did that run on 26 August 2013.

Told you I love these Russian sidecars, in fact so much
I've got three – here's another one.

Chapter 40

If I can't be on a bike, then my second-favourite place in the world to be is in my shed. Sheds are amazing, and so is the relationship that people – well, let's be honest, men – have with their sheds.

The thing about *Shed and Buried* is that it looks like a TV show about fixing up old junk, but it's actually about the psyche of people in sheds and why we love them.

I've been thinking about moving house lately. My neighbour is selling his house and it's nicer than mine. But one of the first things I thought was, I'd be leaving my shed!

So Guy and I have been talking about getting a great big grab, running some straps underneath the shed and sticking it on a low loader. We could just tractor it round there. That's the magic of a shed. You can pick it up and move it.

A good shed ain't cheap, but it's not insanely expensive either.

I always advise potential shed builders that you've really got to be thinking in the five-to-ten-grand region. Spending five hundred quid down at B&Q is fine if you literally want somewhere to store crap that you attach no value to, but for that money you're just going to have some damp, horrible structure you're never going to want to spend any time in, and you'd be better off using the cash to hire a skip.

My first shed cost me five grand. I built it with Guy.

My second shed – the one with the racing Riley in it – that was four and a half. A couple of Kosovans turned up and put it up in an afternoon. They didn't hang the door properly, but everything else they did mint.

For a proper, top-spec shed you've got to have heat and light, so you've got to have power. It's got to be dry, so you need concrete foundations. It's got to be warm, so you can't have flimsy walls. You're going to want to paint it inside. Maybe a few work benches. Carpet on the floor, perhaps? It's got to have everything you have in your house, and then it becomes a place where you want to stay, whether you're working on the bike or not.

So that's ten grand – or build it yourself over a year, which I haven't got time for.

Now, if that sounds like a lot of money, remember, this is your penthouse shed.

I've seen many a shed that was freezing cold, the water was coming in, things were getting wrecked in it, it's a mess and you just don't want to be in it. So you park your bicycle in it and you leave.

I want a shed where I can park the bike, and think, I'll give it a clean. I'll have a sit down and a cup of tea and look at it. I love this bike. A shed where, if someone said to me, 'Henry, sleep in here tonight,' I'd say, 'Fine. Give me a sleeping bag and I'll kip on the floor.'

That's a proper shed. And a proper shed is not a storage facility.

One of the key things about sheds is that they should provide a rust-free environment. Rust is one thing I will not tolerate. And that's the problem with barns. I have never understood those open-sided barns farmers have, with half a million quid's worth of machinery in them, rusting away. You know, wind and rain come sideways, guys. Put a side on.

Barns don't have any soul either. They don't foster male creativity like sheds do. Everything in this world that is worth anything, mechanically-wise, has been invented in a shed.

I mean, think about it. The motor, the electric light bulb, the telephone. Sheds, sheds, sheds.

Who needs a great big working environment and a factory and all that kind of stuff?

A factory is for mass-production. A shed is for one-offs.

Ironically, for such a confined space, a shed is very conducive to intellectual and emotional freedom.

Sheds are also one of the last great hideouts for the male of the species. I've actually never met a female shed owner. I wish I had.

You have to be a bit wary about shed talk – make sure no one's listening because it could be misconstrued if taken out of context. It's free speech in the shed, right. And if it's out of order, someone is going to say, 'That's out of order, Henry, you can't say that, you cunt.' But it's all right in a shed.

You can be you in a shed. You don't have to fake it to be anybody else, like you do sometimes in front of the wife: 'Darling, really? Tell me about that new dress.'

I'm not interested, am I? I mean, let's be honest, I'm not, you know. But I feign interest because I love her, you know.

But in a shed, you can tell someone to piss off.

Emotionally, shed ownership lets me create my own world. It's the same reason I was into model railways as a kid. Sheds are also a sacred space away from the home.

Your wife, or very occasionally, your husband, doesn't get to come into your shed. What goes on in my shed is not subject to the same laws as what goes on in the house. That's her domain; this is mine. I can't wheel a motorbike into the kitchen, but I most definitely can wheel one into my shed. And Janie would never want stuff that I restore in the house. Those lovely lamps I've been working on? They're for sheds as far as she's concerned.

I can wheel a car in.

I can keep a cow in it.

I can try to grow bananas in it.

I can make mistakes in a shed and it doesn't matter.

I can break things in a shed when I'm trying to fix them. On Boxing Day, just to get out of the house, I stripped the carburettor out of a working bike, cleaned it, put it back together and the thing wouldn't start.

Didn't matter. Happened in the shed.

I can do whatever I want in my shed.

In a house there are rules, but there are no rules in a shed.

Lots of people who have one shed find they want to get another.

I was in a shed the other day, and, peering out the window, I saw another one.

I said, 'What's in that shed?'

The geezer went, 'You can't go in there, mate.'

'Oh, right, fair enough,' I said.

But then later, I'd sort of won his trust, and he said, 'Ok, you can have a look through the window into the other shed.'

So I looked through the window, and see his collection of Daleks. Right? So don't think that every shed has an old motorbike in it.

I went to another shed recently. Belonged to this bloke, Ken. He went, 'Do you want to come into my big shed?'

I went, 'Of course, Ken. Let's have a rummage.'

So he threw open the doors, a massive smile on his face, and said, 'What do you reckon? This is what they call breweryana!'

And there were rows and rows of free-standing shelves with Johnnie Walker Red Label paraphernalia on them: tumblers, glasses, jugs, ashtrays. Thousands of them. All Johnnie Walker. From old pubs. Totally fucking worthless.

Magic.

For shed owners, the shed is the repository for the thing that makes you want to carry on living. You go out, you learn your business, you do whatever you do to pay your mortgage. But you've made enough money to get yourself a shed. Right? Where you can escape the world. Go back to the womb.

No one can tell you what to put in your shed. You can put anything that you want in it. You can watch silent movies, and maybe play along on the piano. It just so happens that my sheds are for automotive memorabilia and motorcycles, right. But I'm sure there are people who have S&M sheds. I mean, I haven't met them yet, and I don't really want to come for the weekend, but there probably are.

The shed is your place, and no one comes in without an invite.

Janie wouldn't dream of coming into my shed. Not because she's banned – there's no need for that; she just wouldn't want to. Janie only comes into my shed if I insist that she comes over and looks at a motorbike. I could be in there naked all day long and she would never know (unless she saw the electricity bill).

I can walk in my shed and put on Boney M and no one's going to give a monkey's.

I can put on Showaddywaddy's greatest hits, and I don't have to justify it to my wife. I can swear blind in there, and swear some more and try to fix a bike.

But it's not about the bike. It's about taking yourself to another dimension: utopia, a holy grail.

If the shed is too big, you're going to feel vulnerable. A shed shouldn't be able to fit more than two motorbikes in it at one time: one on the bench, one on the ground. Building a second, third or fourth shed is usually a much better idea than building a megashed. There's no point in having a megashed because it's got no soul.

I go into sheds where the geezer's got sixty tanks. He doesn't spend any time in there because it's a tank store, not a shed, right?

And that's when things go wrong. People who abuse their sheddery.

I'll never forget on *Shed and Buried*, we went to see this guy down in the West Country.

He shows us into his smallest shed. There are about eight cars in it, including a Bentley Blower, a Lagonda, a Ferrari and Donald Healey's personal Austin-Healey. Amazing. probably four to five million quid's worth of cars in there.

So great. That's his shed, where he spends all his time, right.

But then, out the back, I see these . . . warehouses. Great big industrial units.

'What's in there, mate?'

'Oh, nothing I want to sell, boys.'

'Can we take a look anyway?'

'Sure.'

So off we go. We walk into the shed and it is massive. Maybe 165 feet long, 65 feet wide. And there are, maybe, *a hundred* Jaguars in there – 3.8s, saloons, lots of other classic cars, Ford Populars.

He goes, 'Yeah, I drove all those cars in there and parked them up. I collect them.'

Well, he may have driven them in, but the only way they are coming out is with a grab because every single one is rusted through.

He's brought them in in the 50s and the 60s and done *nothing* to them. They are *fucked*. Every single one of the them is *totally fucked*. It's sacrilege.

But even worse, we go into the next shed, which is probably half the size of the first one, and it has got racking and racking and racking filled with NOS – that's 'new old stock' – spare parts from the 50s and 60s, for classic cars, exhaust manifolds, headlights, carburettors – everything.

There are two huge great holes in the ceiling. Water is pouring in and rusting everything. The floor is covered in beautiful oil cans and old petrol pumps. All lying in the mud. I look at him and I say, 'Mate, what about all these parts?'

He goes, 'Oh, I don't want to sell any of that.'

'Well, what are you doing with it?'

He goes, 'Oh, I might need them one day.'

No, you won't, mate, I think. You're eighty. You're not going to need them. All you've done is stopped a whole load of people who were looking for these original parts from being able to buy them. You've just screwed it on a mega scale. For thousands of people. Probably two million quid's worth of parts, lost for ever.

That's what *Shed and Buried* is all about. There are lots of people who've buried shit in the shed – buried it too far, you know.

I always ask people, 'Are you a hoarder or collector?' And they usually answer, 'A bit of both.'

I do have compassion for these people because I'm a hoarder myself. A hoarder of classic motorcycles and automotive memorabilia. So I do believe that collecting is an expression of addiction. I am addicted to collecting. (I was thinking of buying another one last night.) But I try to keep it in check. How many petrol pumps have I got? Ten? How many oil dispensers? Five? I don't need an intervention quite yet.

But the guys with the barns full of rusting cars? I think they need people in.

But you can't reach them. Some of them won't even let us in. I think it is because they feel so guilty that they fucked so many vehicles. Deep down, they feel awful that they've done nothing with what they've got.

How many times do people go, 'I've got to put my hands up, Henry. I bought this to restore it and I ain't got the time. So you can have it for half what I paid for it.'

Those are the people who are catching it early. They're doing the right thing. They're taking a hit while it can still be salvaged.

I do understand the reluctance to let people in. You want to be left alone in your shed. It's not really somewhere you take people.

Sometimes when we're doing *Shed and Buried*, shed owners do a kind of interview with us before they let us in. When we turn up, we go into the kitchen and meet the wife first. We're in their house with our shoes off, right, drinking tea, to see if we're all right to go in the shed. And that's the crazy thing about it. From a predominantly male perspective, letting someone into their shed is like being stripped naked.

I get it. When I let someone in, I am baring my soul to them.

I can fake any old shit at a dinner party but my shed is the real me. It's decorated how I want it to be (not how the wife wants it) and very few people understand that an Adcoids can like mine is as rare as rocking horse shit.

To find a *second* one and be able to buy it is something that basically has made my year.

A shed is about being in touch with yourself. And that's what I've strived for all my life – to try to understand, *who I am.*

And actually, with a bit of time, on your own, in your shed, you can find out.

And if you're talented, you can create something quite incredible in a shed. Like electric light, or the telly. Probably not penicillin, that was made in a lab – but, you know, look at Burt Munro, World's Fastest Indian.

Shed user.

Roald Dahl.

Shed user.

Shakespeare.

Shed user. Or at least, he would have been if they'd had warm sheds back then.

Chapter 41

The real purpose of a shed is to indulge your passion, and in my case, that is restoration.

Restoring anything teaches you so much about yourself. A good restoration project is a microcosm of life. You look at it and you think, That's daunting. Then you go away, you have a cup of tea, you think about it, you avoid it, but ultimately you decide to have a go.

Let's imagine that we're talking about a motorbike – because I usually am.

I'll look at the bike and think, I haven't got the skillset for that; I can't do that. And then someone turns up – like Guy or Sam or Alan Millyard or any of the restorers who work with me on all the TV shows – and they go, 'Why are you having problems with that?'

And I go, 'Well, mate, look at it. Look.' And I slap it and a mudguard falls off.

They say, 'Just take it in bite-sized chunks.'

And that really is the key to a successful restoration project – understanding that it's going to take time; you're not going to be able to do it in three weeks.

So once you've made the decision to go ahead, that's when you take a massive emotional risk and jump in: you start unscrewing bolts. It really is about that moment, that leap. You thinking, Do I strip the carburettor? I don't know how to do it. But, sod it, I'm going to look it up on YouTube and give it a go.

It's odd that we make such a big deal of it in our heads because, really, what's the worst that can happen? You've got to buy a new car because you've unscrewed a load of bolts and it's gone ping? Well, fuck it, you know. The only way to learn in life is to do it. And restoring a motorcycle is all about just having a go.

You are never going to be Sam Lovegrove, the greatest restorer in the world, the first time you strip a carburettor and put it back together again, but you ask any of the greats – they went through years of turmoil not being able to get something going, not even being able to undo a bolt.

Speaking of which, how *do* you undo a bolt? Anyone who doesn't restore, and hasn't got a clue, will come along with a spanner and stand on it and burr off the corners of the bolt, so eventually it has to be angle-ground off because they've destroyed it.

But restoration teaches you another way. You spray it with WD40, you then give it another go. If it still won't move, you pour penetrating oil on it and leave it overnight. Have another go.

Still won't move? Try heating it up with a blow lamp, so it's cherry red, and see if it goes then. If it doesn't, it might when it cools down.

Still nothing? Get the angle-grinder out and cut it off.

There is real fulfilment in achieving your goal when it comes to the restoration and maintenance of a vehicle.

Shed-dwelling and restoring and fettling things are a way of life for me. And the only way you can find out if it's a way of life for you too is to jump in and start a really simple project. Maybe build a light out of an old petrol can, or change the wheels on a push bike. If it's not for you, that's cool. But you might just find that you are one of us shed-dwellers – a person who actually gets incredible fulfilment out of getting a motorcycle and customizing or restoring it yourself over time.

I'm a great believer that it's good for your health too. Restorers and gardeners live longer because they're always looking for that elusive part or waiting for the next season to see how their herbaceous borders look.

And you need that as you get older. I'll never be at the level of Sam or Alan or Guy, and that's why I don't do it on telly, but I could take the head off an engine and have a look. It's just it will take Sam three minutes, rather than three hours, which makes better TV.

The first mechanical object I ever developed a meaningful relationship with was my Grifter bicycle. I didn't restore it, but I maintained and customized it.

I managed to fabricate a bracket which held twin head lamps. And then I found this geezer who was selling battery-powered indicators. So I had indicators on my Grifter, with a white tube to hold the batteries gaffer-taped onto the down tube.

I've always liked to keep things looking mint. My model railway is still perfect. With all the cars I've had over the years – my Triumph Spitfire and all that kind of stuff – I'd tinker with them a bit, but it's only been in the last ten years, working with Sam and Guy and Alan, that I've become ready to take a risk and possibly break something.

I'll probably never be a full-on restorer, but I'm good at certain parts of it, like rattle canning and preparing stuff for spray paint.

I'm also a good test pilot. I can identify little faults in vehicles and that kind of stuff. I could take out a bike Sam's been working on and go, 'Something's wrong with the handlebars,' or, 'It bogs down in fourth'.

There are so many parallels you can draw between doing a restoration and living life.

The critical thing when you are going to embark on a project is to really consider what you are going to restore. Because whatever you choose, it's probably going to be with you for a long time. So it's like picking the right partner in life; no matter how much you want someone by your side, if there are major red flags with that person, you have to stay away. Same as a bike. Frame rotted through? Don't touch it.

But saying that, sometimes your heart rules your head and you decide that although this bird is clearly trouble, she's so gorgeous you are prepared to take the risk. Likewise, I won't worry that trying to get parts for a Sunbeam Deluxe is like trying to find organic rocking horse shit. I love this bike, I'm going to do it.

Both approaches are right in a way. If you have a passion for a motorcycle or a woman, but you know there are problems ahead, you'll get past those issues if the passion and the love for them are deep enough.

If, on the other hand, it's superficial and you don't have a deep and meaningful connection with that motorcycle or that woman, then save yourself the heartache and walk away now.

One great reason to get involved in restoration is to get the motorcycle you had when you were a kid, or the motorcycle you've always hankered after but can't afford.

But the key thing is, 'know thy beast' – by which I mean, do all your research. Get the Haynes manual and the parts book and the maintenance book before you buy it.

Once you've bought your completely inappropriate and knackered subject, you are undoubtedly going to find yourself at an auto jumble.

Auto jumbles are wonderful. They're a nightclub for the over-sixties.

You turn up to an auto jumble with the same sensations you used to have turning up to a party. But rather than thinking the girl of your dreams might be there, you're thinking, there could just be a 20s V-twin engine here that no one else has seen; you could find that new head lamp for your WLC.

The excitement is endless.

Why? Simple.

If you go to John Lewis or Waitrose, you know exactly what you're going to find. If you go to an auto jumble, you could find anything – a stuffed rat in a glass cabinet, a Fabergé egg or the pistons for your Spitfire.

But most especially, what you're definitely going to find are kindred spirits and people who have the same interests as you. You're not going to be lonely at an auto jumble. You can bore the shit out of 3000–4000 people at the Netley auto jumble, and they can bore the shit out of you. And that's exactly what I like about it.

Tea and coffee are fully available. There're burger vans and all that caper.

If you haven't been to an auto jumble, you haven't lived, because they are what life is all about.

They're about keeping rooted, keeping your feet on the ground. Auto-jumble people don't want a brand new kitchen and a big house in the country. They are just looking for that elusive spragget washer that they've spent two years trying to find. Then they get back to the shed, get the tea on, put the heater on and they fit that part. And it fits! Holy smoke, it fits!

That's the holy grail. That's true happiness.

On the flip side, I've had restorations where I look at them once I've finished and think, Why the fuck did I do that?

Take my street fighter. I spent fifteen thousand quid on that bike with the craziest paint job – the craziest thing that you've ever seen in your life. Could I sell it for that? No.

But it's when it goes wrong, that's when you really learn. You feel so shitty about yourself. You really thought you had an idea about how that bike was going to come together, but you powder coated the frame wrong and the headlight just doesn't look right. It makes you feel awful that you messed it up. But you learn.

I think if you embark on a resto and you get stuck, the way you respond to that is a key test of your character.

Let's say you've stripped the engine on that Honda Melody and you've lost five or six bits of it – ask for professional help. The worst thing you can do is to sit there in your shed on your own, trying to fathom it out. Take it to a Honda specialist, tell them you've fucked it up and ask how to fix it. Then learn from it.

Or, if you've really hit a barrier on rebuilding the gearbox and you haven't got a clue about it, then leave it and move on. It's incredible how if you leave something for a few days and go on to something else, when you come back to the bit that flummoxed you, it comes together real quick.

And if things are just going to shit, take time out from it. Walk away for a few days. Come back to it with fresh eyes. Bring your mate in – because there's nothing better than assembling or restoring something with a friend. That's really exciting. The ideal thing is to have one bike that you're doing and one that he (or she) is doing on another bench. And you restore the two bikes together. That's a relationship made in heaven in my view.

The critical thing is to try to identify a vehicle that you have almost enough knowledge to deal with and not too much to learn, otherwise you're just going to end up frustrated.

First time round, get something like a Hillman Minx or an Imp – a pretty basic car with a plentiful supply of spares, or a little early BSA, which is the perfect bike to start on.

Don't get yourself a complex car, so that you get bogged down, you lose faith and then it becomes a stalled project, as they are called on eBay. You don't want to be a stalled project. It's bad for your psyche.

You need to set yourself up, emotionally, physically and spiritually, with the right challenge.

1942 WLC Harley Davidson

The one specific restoration that I'm very proud of is my WLC Harley Davidson, 1942 bobber. The first thing I did was talk to the owner's club, which is a good tip when doing any resto because they'll tell you what to look out for when you're buying your new project. Also, they'll tell you how to get hold of parts – because there are specific people who make parts for specific brands and you need to know all this before you start.

If there isn't a decent supply of parts because you're restoring something really rare, you need to know someone who can fabricate the parts for you. Now, I'm lucky enough whether it's Alan Millyard, whether it's Guy, whether it's Sam, they can fabricate and create anything, but for most people that's where the owners' clubs come in.

We found this WLC Harley in a shed in Cornwall when we were making *Shed and Buried*. It was a shitter, to be honest. It had been bobbered by someone else, but he'd done it really badly. I mean, like, atrociously: he had put a disc brake on the front, he had cut the head stock to rake it out more, to make it more of a chopper.

So at first, Sam and I walked away and left the bike. But I couldn't get it out of my head. The WLC, or WLA Harley – the WLC was Canadian, the C was for 'Canada' and WLA was for 'Army' – was the instigator of the whole bobber, chopper and customizing scene.

So we went back and got it two years later. The restoration immediately hit a massive problem and that was the head stock, which someone had cut open in a misguided effort to rake out the front wheel. We couldn't find a replica to switch it out for, so we had to cut open the head stock, take the slug of metal out and put it back to the correct geometry. Because Sam is so skilled, that worked really nicely, and has actually come out great.

The thing about restoration is that it's so spiritually uplifting is to confront your fears. We had a situation with that frame where the easy thing to do would have been to switch out the head stock part of the frame and go and get a new part and put it in, but we really pushed ourselves and saved the original.

Spiritually, you know, taking the windy road in resto and in life is often more difficult, but so much more rewarding. Taking the decision to fix this head stock was a risk. But people like us just insist on keeping the original stuff – keep the original wheels, the original spokes and have them all refurbished – because it becomes a way of life.

You may be sitting there dreaming of your next HP purchase of a Ferrari, but trust me, you'll get so much more satisfaction and contentment finding that head stock or that set of spokes for your BSA Bantam for a hundred quid at the Netley Marsh auto jumble. That's what it's all about. It's so fulfilling; not for anybody else, but for you.

And it doesn't matter what you're restoring – whether it's a lawn-mower or a 1946 American pick-up. When it's done, you'll sit back and you'll go, 'Wow, man. That's just so gorgeous.' And, more importantly, you'll feel gorgeous about yourself too.

Chapter 42

My fascination with restoration reached its pinnacle when we set about creating the Gladstone motorcycle.

Since we were fifteen, Guy and I have always loved the same kind of bikes, and one of the manufacturers I always loved was a guy called Ian Barry, who ran Falcon Motorcycles in Los Angeles.

Ian's bikes sell for about a quarter of a million bucks, and he builds one or two a year. They're unbelievable.

The particular one that I saw was one of his prototypes, and it was a bobber.

Guy and I have always been into bobbers. Bobbers are bikes with no front mudguard. They really appeal to me because they grew out of social history. After World War II, no one could afford to buy a civilian bike because they were far too expensive, so instead they were buying all the Harleys that were coming back from the front and being sold off for very little money. Then, to make them look a bit more civilian, they'd cut the mudguards off. This also took a lot of the weight off them, so they were faster for racing.

That was called bobbing a bike and it became a custom style. The bobber then became the chopper, as designers extended the front forks.

Anyway, I saw this Ian Barry bobber and I thought that I'd love to build something like that. I really felt there was a market for a super high-end, retro, custom British bobber.

I rang up Guy who I hadn't seen for a bit.

I said to him, 'Look, I want to start manufacturing bikes.' I sent him the picture, and said, 'I want to do something like that.'

And he said, 'I love it, mate. That would just be amazing.'

'Great, ok. Well, what are you doing?'

'Oh, I'm being a plumber in Cambridge.'

I said, 'Look, mate, back in those dark heroin days you saved my life. So don't be a plumber any more, come and work for me.'

And he did.

Together, we created this chassis to drop an engine into. We created this bike and our premise was: if, when we pulled the sheet off it at the show, there is even one tiny bit of it that we hated, we would put the sheet back on and go back to square one.

So over a two-year period, we made this bike together. Guy built it and I designed it with him. And in that whole period, we didn't argue once.

And suddenly we had a prototype, and we started selling them.

I named them Gladstone after Redbeard. Because he had got me into bikes in the first place. It felt like a way to carry on his legacy.

We say Gladstone is for the discerning hooligan, which sums up me and my kind of people who understand and love motorcycles.

The 'discerning' bit refers to the fact they're thirty-five thousand quid plus the VAT. We still lose a ton of money on them – it takes Guy three months to build one, so thirty-five thousand quid really is nothing. You don't make money out of selling low volume bikes.

The whole Gladstone brand sums up everything about me; it kind of encapsulates my strange life, that bike. Everything on it we made ourselves. Everyone said we should just get parts from other manufacturers and bolt them on.

Well, no. No.

I've got to follow my own route in life, so consequently, it took fourteen months to develop a speedo when we could have gone out and bought one.

We wanted to get to a stage where we could build the prototype and then give it to a manufacturer to carry on and we'd take a percentage of the bikes' sales. And that's exactly what's now happened with Norton. They are producing fifty Commando specials with us, and seeing them roll off the production line is going to be one of the proudest moments of my life.

We set out to build nine Gladstone number ones and we have sold them all. I think we have achieved our goal of building the quintessential British bobber.

Building a custom motorcycle is where my lifelong passion and love for bikes really crystallized. It wasn't about the custom scene in the sense of radical high bars and all that kind of stuff, but the evolution of the custom motorcycle.

That's what rows my boat. Motorcycling to me is about soul, it's about making a statement and it's about the love and hunger for bare-bones motorcycling.

I don't want heated seats and heated grips and all that bollocks.

I want the philosophy.

I want to uphold and embrace the philosophy of minimalist, bare-arsed biking, and the greatest interpretation of that in the custom scene is a bobber. So that's what Guy and I set out to do.

Of course, if we knew then what we know now, we would never have done it the way we did it.

When I told Stuart, the boss at Norton, that I wanted to make nine identical bespoke motorcycles of the highest quality, and that I wanted to build, design and manufacture every last bit of the bikes – my own speedo, my own headlight, my own petrol tank, my own fender, my own everything – Stuart looked at me and he went, 'Are you an idiot?'

And I went, 'What do you mean by that?'

'If you get involved in manufacturing and designing your own headlights, speedo, etcetera, it will be a nightmare,' he explained. 'Why don't you just go into the parts catalogues and buy the parts? No one will ever know that basically this bike is a collection of parts that you have styled the way that you want.'

I went, 'Fuck off, Stuart. I'm going to do it my way,' which he respected. And Guy and I proceeded to do just that.

Three years later, we actually had a motorcycle that we were proud of. It wasn't made with parts we had bought and bolted together. That would have been a six-month project.

We stupidly decided to create every single component on that bike that we could, and blueprint an old Triumph engine to go in it.

Consequently, we set ourselves on a journey that has been, at times, the most unrewarding challenge you could possibly give yourself.

When I went to Bonneville I met Jay Leno through Sammy, and I told him about it.

He said, 'Sorry, say that again?'

And I went, 'We're going to make nine bikes.'

He said, 'Sorry, man, what? Nine identical bikes?'

I went, 'Yeah.'

'Made by British people?'

'Yeah.'

'Man,' he said. 'British people only make one-offs. You're fucked.'

And he was right. Because British manufacturers are brilliant at prototyping stuff, but actually to make, whether it's nine or 900 headlights which are all the same, but bespoke, it's a nightmare to find the right people to do it.

We had to go out to the marketplace and search for the people who could do it. Let's take the speedo, for example. I wanted it to be an homage to the 5-inch 150-mile-an-hour speedo on a Vincent. Our interpretation of a real classic.

It took us fourteen months to get that design right. We went through thirty speedos. Cost me probably about five to eight grand. We could have bought one off the shelf and stamped Gladstone on the face, but we're not in the business of that.

What we wrestled with on the speedo were two elements: the fascia and the mechanics within it and the casing.

The mechanics of it were easy, because they're just standard, but what I wanted for the fascia just seemed to be impossible for anyone to understand. I thought it was simple. All I wanted was a fascia with the Gladstone Griffin in the middle of it, the right font for the numbers and a needle with a pear-drop end to it, which was pointed rather than squared off.

But I must have got fifteen different interpretations of that fascia, all of which were total crock and not what I'd asked for in the first place.

Once we had the front fascia right, and we had the needle right, we then obviously had to create the case, the housing for it, and that was milled out of billet metal. And that was all fine, except that in the wet it leaked because the rubber O-rings weren't quite right and then the speedo kept reading ridiculous speeds; calibrating it took for ever.

In the end, we nailed it. CAI Smith Gauges came through and sorted it out and the guys at Fastech created the casing. But I've got to tell you, I could have bought a speedo for four hundred quid off the shelf which looked vaguely like ours and put a badge on it.

I'm so glad we didn't.

One amazing thing is that throughout the whole process over the last five years, Guy and I have never argued about styling – and the reason for that is because we both come from the same aesthetic background. So when it actually came to building our interpretation of a bobber, there was never any argument.

For example, how do you mount the rear mudguard? Does it end before the spindle? Does it end after the spindle? Does it go all the way round?

I just put the mudguard on the rear tyre to where I thought it should end, which was right at the apex of the wheel, so it didn't go all the way round the back. Then we both looked at it and went, 'That's it. Happy days.'

It's the same with the tank. We knew exactly what we wanted and how we wanted to sculpt it to have a good bit of bobber influence.

We've never had any discussion last longer than a few minutes. Alan Sugar once said to me, 'Henry, just remember this: if a meeting goes past twenty minutes long, it's based on ego.'

He's absolutely right. Meetings only drag on – whether it's designing a motorcycle or deciding how many staff you're going to have – because someone likes the sound of their own voice. When you're actually developing and creating something with a mate, you don't care about that shit; you get down to the nitty gritty straight away.

The whole thing about collaboration is not to have an ego in it.

And to have someone working with you who you respect and love dearly is amazing. We never raise our voices to each other because we value each other's judgment and we also know what we particularly love about a motorcycle.

Another example: we very much wanted the bike to have a statement headlight. We looked at vintage car headlights as a creative steer. What we both loved was a metal tri-bar, over the lens, with a knurled headlight ring round it.

We set about designing that from billet and got Fastech to machine it and that came out really well.

So we got a billet ring, three rings of knurled edging round the rim of the headlight and it's got a perfect vintage look. It was crucial, really, because the headlight is a bike's signature.

With a bike, no one really looks at the engine straight off. It's the whole stance of the thing – the headlight, the tank and the seat – that hits you first.

So if those don't work, you might as well go home.

We wanted period front forks, so we went through a load of fork options, and ultimately settled on replica Ceriani ones; they're Italian-made but part of British design history.

On the front wheel, we didn't want a disc brake on it, so we looked again at what we really loved, and we settled on a four leading shoe front hub (a Ceriani replica again) to match the forks.

That front hub took us so long, but there's a great satisfaction in knowing that every single component on a bike is unequivocally the very best.

Our founding decision – that if we were to pull off the sheet to reveal the bike and see one thing, even a wing mirror or a brake rod that wasn't right, we'd put the sheet back on and go back to the drawing board – was crucial. We stuck to it and, as a result, we go into so much detail on the Gladstones: every single bolt that goes on the bike is either made by us or the manufacturer's stamp is ground off, so it looks old and period.

The only thing that we actually haven't made or designed ourselves are the levers, which are from my mate Alessandro in Florence – because they're already the most beautiful levers in the world.

The key for us was always to find and engage with the best craftsmen in the UK and that's why it has taken five years to find those people and use them – like Paul, who does the seats (he does all the Formula 1 seats).

Then came the engine. We were both obsessed with the engines out of Triumph T140s from the 1970s. So we got those (which cost me in rough state about fifteen hundred quid), then we sent them up to Dick at Baron's Speed Shop, who we believe is one of the best at rebuilding Triumph engines (he charged another five grand for the rebuild). We could have put in a modern engine at about fifteen hundred quid a go. But no, no, we spent six and a half thousand quid in total, blueprinting an old engine, so it's brand new.

Such are the lengths that we went to. And people wonder why the bike's thirty-five grand.

But now it's all paying off – we're building specials for clients. We've also designed a body kit for the Norton 961 Commando. Norton asked us to create a different look for that model, so we changed the body kit, we changed the tank, we changed the exhaust pipe, we changed the bars and we made it look like an old/new 80s superbike.

I think there is a really exciting future for us with Gladstone Motorcycles. We are experimenting with the idea of being a design house, rather than an actual manufacturing business for motorcycles. And so far it's worked really well. Norton released fifty of those – they're called the 961 Street – and they've sold out. And we're in discussions with other manufacturers too.

That might be the future for Gladstone, but we will also continue building one-off specials, going for and breaking land speed records at Bonneville and here in the UK for vintage classes. Think tweed-suit, handle-bar moustache, discerning hoodlum and nuttery and that is our DNA.

Even if I never make my money back, the point is I am insanely proud of Gladstone.

It's my legacy.

Guy and I have built what we believe to be the best bobber in the world. And as long as we are alive – and who knows how long that may be for a couple of old ex-junkies – we'll have this: *we did it.*

Chapter 43

When you present *World's Greatest Motorcycle Rides*, people, understandably enough, sometimes ask you, 'Henry, what is the greatest motorbike ride of all time?'

The real answer, as every motorcyclist knows, is probably that random morning on the B987654321 when you'd just got that new job you'd always wanted, pulled that bird or bloke you'd always fancied, the temperature was perfect and the sun was just coming up. Because what happened that morning is that you were in the perfect emotional state, and although you only rode 50 miles on a poxy 125, you were right there in the elements, the skies, the moment and it encapsulated every single reason why you got into motorcycling in the first place.

The Buddhists have never had to work very hard to convince us motorcyclists that it's all about the journey. And, to be totally honest, the concerning thing about your big ride of a lifetime that you save up for two years to go and do, is that you book yourself on a tour to do Route 66 and you turn up at the hotel and they're all a bunch of tossers.

You arrive at the hotel in Chicago, it's pissing with rain and there's a bloke called Kelvin and his wife, Deirdre, who could win the 800-metre boring straight away. And you're left with them on a table while everyone is being introduced by this absolute knob of a tour guide who you realize, by about eleven o'clock on the first night, is a prat of the first order. And you've got to spend two weeks with him.

You wake up the next morning, you look out the window, and it's still pissing with rain. You also find out that you're picking up the Harley in east Chicago, which means that you've got to ride with twenty other people, who probably can't ride as well as you, through Chicago in rush hour in the rain before you can even think about being on Route 66.

So with that in mind, and assuming, for the sake of argument, that the sun is shining and you've a following wind, and the tour guide doesn't have life-ending halitosis, Route 66, as discussed previously, has to be done.

And if I was only allowed to ever ride a bike twice more in my life, the second trip would be to New Zealand.

New Zealand, to me, is one of the most incredible places on this planet to ride a motorcycle for many reasons.

Firstly, there ain't a straight road in New Zealand. It is bends galore. But not those switchback bends that people go on about. ('Oh yeah, I love riding the switchbacks over the Alps.' Do you, mate? Really? Why? You're either going really slowly and taking in the views or you're not seeing anything, and you come round the corner and there's gravel on it. It's hairpin after hairpin after hairpin. I find it unpleasant.)

No, in New Zealand you're going through these unbelievably beautiful mountains, you're cruising, taking in the views. You set yourself up for a bend, you stick your leg out and the bend ain't going to do anything apart from what it says on the tin. It's not suddenly going to tighten up on you. The road's not suddenly going to go to shit and reveal a massive pothole.

And the real magic is: there's no one there. It's a country with the same land mass as the UK, but we've got 66 million of us fuckers here, whereas New Zealand has 4.5 million, 3.2 million of whom live in Auckland. So the South Island is sporadic, shall we say, in terms of population.

Another great thing about New Zealand is that when it comes to the culture, to me as a tourist anyway, they seem to have good integration between the Māori and the non-indigenous sides of life, as opposed to Australia, where it can all feel a bit forced and fake.

In New Zealand, you really feel as though there is a rich culture that you can embrace as a tourist and be part of. I'm sure there are mass murderers out there and all that stuff, but I've never met a wrong 'un there, and I've been riding in NZ four times.

I suggest you fly into Auckland because it's easy to get to, then head down to Wellington, and cross on the ferry at Picton to the South Island.

The South Island is like Scotland on acid, blown up to 50,000 times the size. I mean the mountains are just extraordinary. The whole time, you're going, 'Holy shit! Look at that!'

And the roads! They are massively wide – what would pass for A-roads here, all of them. Plus, there are no potholes in New Zealand, from what I've seen.

The only tiny downer is that on the west side they measure the rainfall in metres, not inches. So you do get a little bit wet.

The natural environment is what it's all about though, really. You go through these forests, and you think a dinosaur is going to come out at you any moment. Everywhere you stop, some geezer comes up and goes, 'You know what, mate, *Lord of the Rings* was filmed over here.'

They must have moved around a hell of a lot. I mean, Peter Jackson must have blown the budget on trucks, if you know what I mean. But you believe them because it's just so beautiful.

You go to places like Wanaka and Queenstown. Queenstown is on the edge of the world, but you feel as though you're in Soho, because it's a little movie capital, where all the studios are, and it's really trendy and hip with cool restaurants.

But you're on the arse end of the planet! Next stop is Antarctica.

Another great thing about New Zealand, for me as a motorcyclist, is Invercargill, the birthplace of Burt Munro. Herbert James 'Burt' Munro, known as the world's fastest Indian, was a New Zealand motorcycle racer, famous for setting an under-1000cc world record on an 'Indian' bike, at Bonneville on 26 August 1967, which still stands.

He was sixty-eight and riding a forty-seven-year-old machine when he set his last record, and Hayes, a hardware shop in the city, funded him to go and do it.

It's real David-and-Goliath stuff.

There is a beach at Invercargill, called Oreti beach, where Burt tested his bikes, and to this day, you can go down there and ride your bike on it. I've ridden down it. It's hard packed and it goes on for just over 12 miles. And obviously, because there's very few people, as previously noted, the chance of running over a small child with candy floss in their hand is minimal.

Burt had a Velocette as well and he held the land speed record for that bike (which is actually in the hardware store still).

It's real history. You feel it in the atmosphere; you experience the tingle down your spine.

I don't think there are any traffic lights in New Zealand, outside of the cities. When you're out and about, you're not going to see anything like that. No cops. Nothing. And there's so many things to do. I'm not a touristy person, but it's brilliant.

So you need to do New Zealand.

Next up, for an incredible sense of solitude, go to Australia. But do not, whatever you do, ride up the east coast – unless you really want to meet a million backpackers.

I have ridden from Sydney via Melbourne and Adelaide to Perth and from Perth up the west coast to Darwin.

Both of those are coast-to-coast trips; east coast to west coast and then west coast to north.

Riding across the Nullarbor plain, from east to west, is 2000 miles of straight road. That road has the longest straight on the planet, at 95 miles. It's insane. When the straight breaks, it moves by, say, 1 degree and then carries on like that for another 500 miles or something.

I did it on a Harley, on cruise control. I rarely touched the handlebars – because you can corner by sticking your leg out and the resistance turns the bike.

You will die on the Nullarbor plain if you ride at dawn or dusk because there are half a million wild camels sharing the space with you. There are also kangaroos, wombats and emus. Emus are just the right height and build to kill a motorcyclist: long, spindly legs and a massive body right at the level of your chest and head. They gather at dawn on the edges of the road where the water gullies are and then they get spooked by you and jump onto the road and kill you.

A road train guy said to me once, 'If I hit a camel, I'm fucked. If I hit a kangaroo, it just goes dum-dum. If I hit a sheep, I'm fucked.'

I asked, 'Why a sheep?'

'Because,' he explained, 'they explode when we hit them, and all their wool gets wrapped around the wheels, so we have to take a day out to clean all the wool off.'

Cows write off the trucks as well. Three tons of steak hitting the grill.

When I was riding Perth to Darwin, which is a 6500-mile trek, I flew into Oz from Kuala Lumpur. I was looking out of my little window and below me there was red earth. That's all I could see. Apart from a straight white line.

And I was looking out of that window for five hours.

Red earth.

White line.

Just as we're coming into Perth I realized what it was.

It was the road.

It took me *three weeks* to ride on a bike.

You have no concept, in normal life, of the loneliness you feel out on those roads. An old biker once said to me that loneliness breeds solitude and solitude breeds serenity.

In that case, if you want to find serenity, ride round Australia. Because the only person you've got to talk to is yourself. That's why, after doing the east-to-west coast trip, I went back and did the west coast up to the north because I wanted to experience that loneliness, that nothingness, that isolation.

Once you've experienced that and you're stuck in the middle of town on a Friday night with a load of people who really want to go to the Piano and Pitcher, you just think, What is this world all about?

It's good for self-reliance, that trip. You obviously have to take water and a few cans of petrol, because it's about 350 miles between petrol stations.

What's interesting about the petrol stations is that there's absolutely nothing there, apart from undoubtedly the worst hotel you have ever seen (until the next day). And this a hotel where there is no need for any customer service what-soever because you've got no alternative but to stay there. They only have about twenty rooms in each one, and they are always booked up. So if you don't have a reservation, you're on the gravel, you're camping. They do burgers and chips and that's it, and some of them are proper shitholes. Breeze blocks with strip lighting and a bed. Not very cool in a country where everything is trying to kill you. That's Aussie roadhouses for you.

So Australia is the most incredible place, a real adventure, and you have to go there if at all possible.

Talking of adventure, the third best place to ride a motorcycle is South Africa.

Now, when you say you are going to South Africa everyone will tell you you're going to get shot. Well, I don't get that. I've been out there riding about four times and I've never met a dude who's nasty. Never.

You go out into the villages, you pull the bike up and they're all round – they're chatting, they're lovely, they're really happy to see you.

I've seen quite a bit of Soweto coming up over the years. What an amazing place it is now! I was there recently for a *World's Greatest Motorcycle Rides*.

South Africa is incredible because of the dichotomy of landscape. You've got great mountain riding, you've got desert riding, you've got some of the best off-road riding. The Garden Route – which is Cape Town down to Port Elizabeth – I call that South Africa light. But if you're planning a first big ride, then I would heartily recommend it because you are still riding South Africa. You're properly involved but, you're going to be all right, son.

Most recently, I did Jo'burg to Cape Town through the Kalahari. That's a little bit more hardcore. It is the most phenomenal place and it's also as much about the people and the culture. The wildlife is amazing too, but the problems with it are really distressing. I mean, I have big problems around that. The conservation problem, on the ground it is not good.

For example, they're killing three rhinos a day. I was riding up near the Kruger National Park and got talking to some top geezers about it. They say that you can't really blame some bloke in Mozambique (which has an open border with the Kruger National Park) who is living in a container, who can't feed his family and is told, 'Go and get me a rhino. Bring back the horn, I'll give you $5,000.' It's going to change his life. Who gives a fuck about the rhino? So they come across the border, and, you know, eventually they get a rhino.

But I'm told it's not actually about 'saving the rhino', it's about saving the ecosystem too. That's the real problem.

In Kruger, they're poisoning the vultures, because the vultures give away where the carcasses are, so potentially give a clue to a helicopter team to get there to then find the poachers who haven't been able to get away.

But then lions and leopards get snared or shot because they're eating the farmer's livestock. One of the solutions discussed on the ground, to deal with it long term, is to turn the farmland back into natural ecosystem and then allow people to shoot big game; not lions but buffalo and all that kind of stuff that are pretty easy to breed.

Not popular with the Islington lot, that.

But back to the biking. South Africa has everything you could possibly want as a motorcyclist. Especially if you're into dual sport – the on-road, off-road stuff.

There are hundreds of thousands of miles of that and the weather's normally great. You can easily hire bikes out there. The touring's awesome, and the people who do it are too. Plus, an added bonus: everyone speaks English.

What's more, the people are insanely resourceful.

We had a problem in South Africa with our Métisse. (In hindsight, attempting to ride an old British bike from Johannesburg to Cape Town through the Kalahari Desert was stupid, especially as I hadn't really explained to Gerry, the guy in the factory, exactly what I was going to use the bike for.)

So I start fudding off on this Métisse, Steve McQueen replica, a 650 Triumph with an old 60s TR6 engine in it.

Ok.

So I'm riding along, and the thing basically starts to fall apart.

I've got oil leaking, I've got shock absorbers that are sheared off. I've got electrics that aren't really working properly and I've got no rubber left on the tyres. They have just worn away.

I'm in Kuruman, in the middle of nowhere in South Africa in the Kalahari. I take the wheels off to try to find out what the fuck's going on and realize we need to replace the shock absorbers. But where do you find shock absorbers in the middle of nowhere?

Well, our fixer, Ghonze, he sees a guy on a Harley Davidson, right. The geezer's outside his front door with a Harley. So what does Ghonze do? He asks to buy the guy's shock absorbers off his Harley. The guy unbolts them and sells them to us, right there and then. We shoe-horn them onto the bike and they kind of fit; the wheel's jacked up a little bit in the air but, you know, we have a result. That keeps us going until we discover that there are no more tyres of the right size to fit the Métisse in the whole of South Africa, so we have to abandon it and call in the help of KTM, who sort us with a 990 Adventure.

We got my Métisse fixed eventually and it's back in the shed with a load of memories. It's one of my favourite bikes to ride.

There are a few health risks in such far-flung places. Last time I was in Africa, Alex Jackson, a tour guide I ride with, told me: 'You won't believe what happened to me the other day, Henry.'

'What?' I asked.

'Well, I started to sweat and I thought my mother was with me and she died twenty-one years ago. I thought I had malaria. I went to the doctor, I had all these blood tests. I couldn't stand up, my whole life was fucked. And the doctor said, "You haven't got malaria, you've got African tick fever. You've been bitten by a tick. Take these really strong antibiotics and you'll be all right." And I was.'

Now, I'm such a hypochondriac. I mean, if I find a blister on my tongue, it's cancer. If my heart's gone out of rhythm, I'm having a heart attack.

So I was sitting in this five-star lodge on the phone to Janie and I saw this tick stuck on me. I hung up on Janie and got on the phone to the lodge geezer at midnight saying, 'I've got tick fever!'

He said, 'Look, mate, Henry, please . . . I've got bitten by about a thousand ticks.'

'Oh, all right,' I said. 'So I'm ok, then?'

'Of course you're ok,' he laughed.

Anyway, I started to go down on the last week of the job. I was just getting on the flight when I started getting the shits and sweating. But I got on the plane, took three Imodiums and didn't shit for a week.

Anyway, guess what? My leg came up like a balloon and I had tick fever!

So sometimes the hypochondriac in me is right.

1952 Reliant Three-Wheeler

This three-wheel delivery van from 1952 was the original LDV. It's got a motorcycle front end with a pick-up back. Now, the joy of that was that a sixteen-year-old delivery boy on a motorcycle licence could drive it. They didn't have to get a car licence. Consequently, it was the go-to back in the late 40s, early 50s for butchers, ironmongers, all sorts. Of course, it's also the forerunner to the Reliant Robin – but that's where it all went wrong as far as I am concerned.

It's the craziest thing to drive. It's got an Austin 7 engine in it –750cc.

It really sums me up, this motor. It's socially unacceptable, pretty ugly, but so eccentric and idiosyncratic that you've got to own one.

When you drive along, people just look at you open-mouthed. Who invented that? Where did that come from?

And to me, that's what it's about. It's about entertaining people with what you're driving, rather than making them feel jealous that you've got some flash sports car. It cruises at 20, and I take it out on high days and holidays. All I hope is that when I'm dead and gone this Reliant will still be rocking.

Motor museums are fantastic, and I love a good one, but only briefly – because we all know where a motorcycle or a car should be, even if that's only once a year.

You've got to take it out and give it a run, to let other people see it working and bore someone shitless in a petrol station.

Chapter 44

A bit closer to home, one of the greatest bike rides in Europe is the Balkans, starting in Ljubljana, Slovenia, then down to Croatia, Bosnia, Serbia and Bulgaria. Croatia is like Italy without the hordes of crazy car drivers.

The last time I was there before I went in 2015 was during the Bosnian war, so you can imagine it was indescribably amazing to see it again, but at peace.

The roads are big, wide and predictable. The road surface is great. The weather's fantastic, the food's brilliant and it's just like Italy without the hassle.

I love Italian culture and all that, don't get me wrong, but you ride through Split, and it's like a miniature Rome without the tourists.

You can also go island-hopping on the bikes. There are ferries every two seconds and the crossing's only ten minutes. So Slovenia–Croatia is just one of the best places to ride. And it's cheap to get there too.

It gets a bit more adventurous if you go on down, because you're going Bosnia, Serbia, Bulgaria and you could go on down to Istanbul. But I stopped at Sofia in Bulgaria and flew home.

As I said, going back to Bosnia was one of the most extraordinary things ever. I went to Mostar and last time I was there, right at the end of the war in 1995, I was in my flak jacket with a load of shit going on; someone was always firing at someone.

But riding into Sarajevo, where I'd spent time, I was crying my eyes out. I didn't see the real shit in the war, but I was there for the end; I was there for Richard Holbrooke coming in for the Dayton Accords and filming those mass graves.

So crazy.

An hour and a half flight from London and no one gave a shit.

It was massively emotional.

Going into Serbia I felt very uneasy, just riding in there. But, weirdly, what I found was that when you got down into the country, deep Serbia was untouched by the war, really. It was just where they were fighting on the border and around Sarajevo that was wrecked.

The further I went, the more I felt I was stepping back from it, away from that part of my history, letting it go.

Spain is amazing and very accessible. Just catch the ferry to Santander and pin it. It's one of the secret places to ride in Europe, central and southern Spain and the desert outside Almería.

There's nothing on the road, the road surfaces are normally pretty good, the weather is insanely gorgeous and the scenery, food and people are incredible.

Spain has a never-ending supply of glorious roads. You really don't have to spend a lot of money to have the greatest rides of your life.

Also, what is really good is enduro-riding in central Spain.

Europe is just full of the most beautiful riding. If you were to ride from here through France, down through Spain, stop for a fag in Puerto Banús and come back up, then that is just the most beautiful trip.

There are so many things to find in Europe. The minute you get out of this nanny state of ours, you know, people actually respect and understand motorcycling so much more.

Chapter 45

If I was going on a really local motorcycle adventure, there are a few clear winners for me in the UK.

The A272, which goes from Winchester in Hampshire to Billingshurst is maybe not that good as a road *per se*, but it was my father's favourite road to drive in his Morris van, collecting antiques, because he liked moonlighting as an antique dealer. He loved that road so much. It is a biker's road, but they've put speed cameras up and the pigs are there all day long, nicking people.

Dad's dying wish was that he be buried on the A272, right. So I had to bung the vicar large in a village called Bramdean to drop him in a little pot in a churchyard that overlooks the A272.

I went back about ten years ago and couldn't find his grave. I don't know where it's gone. All these bushes have grown over it because he refused to have a headstone. So my father has officially disappeared, which may pose a problem when my mother turns up her toes because I won't know where to bury her. I'll have to go down to Bramdean and rustle around on my hands and knees with a strimmer to find him.

So that, to me, for various reasons, is an iconic road.

One of the greatest roads to ride in the UK on a sunny day is on the north coast of Scotland – John O'Groats to Ullapool. You can't believe you are in the UK: azure-blue water, sandy beaches, beautiful roads with no one on them. It is mesmeric.

Wales is a joy too – all round the Brecon Beacons. And the Yorkshire Dales are stunning. Generally, the more remote, the better, as there are fewer tin boxes.

I love getting on a KTM 1190 and riding from London to Istanbul. But, on the other hand, I've also got a Hudson Auto-cycle, a 98cc, pedal-powered moped, and last weekend I rode 18 miles to Bibury at 20 miles per hour – and sometimes that's enough to keep you thinking life is bloody amazing.

The other great thing about biking in the UK is the cafés. They are the last place in the world safe from smashed avocado and quinoa. The staple for us bikers when we go out to a café is a full English. On the one hand, we should be given a better option for food and a better option for our surroundings, but on the other, thank God we ain't.

The food is standard issue. We're straight-up people.

We don't want any fucking sugar-free baked beans.

We don't want any fucking salads.

At least, I don't.

I mean, I just want sausage, egg, chips and beans wherever I go in the world.

You know, we go to places like the Ace Café, and the reason we go there is because of the camaraderie. You turn up to the Ace Café because it was iconic in the 50s and everyone turns up there and you want to see their bikes and chat with them and all that kind of stuff.

I guarantee you: no one's going to catch a Tube to the Ace Café for lunch.

1928 Boat Tail Riley Racer

This is a 1928 Riley, rebodied in the 50s to be a boat tail racer, which had a starring role in a book called *Dear Lupin: Letters to a Wayward Son*, which I loved. *Dear Lupin* is a book of letters between John Mortimer and his wayward son, Charlie. The story that reveals itself in the letters is amazing, and I really related to it because a lot of it was about addiction and his struggle with drugs. The letters reminded me so much of my father on the phone to me. So I couldn't believe it when this car, which they talk about a lot in the letters, turned up in the yard of a dealer mate called Anthony Godin.

I hankered after it for about a year and a half before finally buying it.

I swapped it for a motorbike and a heap of cash.

It had been raced up until the 60s, and then it had gone to Malta, where it did the odd rally. It was restored again, but it never ran properly. Anthony was very straight up about that. He said to me, 'Henry, it doesn't run right – you know that.'

I got it home on a trailer and just looked at it for a while. Then I asked Sam to take a look.

'Try and start it, Henry,' he said, and he looked into the bonnet.

'It won't start, Sam. It doesn't start, that's the point.'

Sam went, 'That's because the rotor arm of the distributor is going the wrong way. Order a new distributor.'

So I did. I ordered it that morning and it turned up in the afternoon. We went to pick it up from the store – a racing place, in Chippenham. He put it in, and now she runs like a Swiss watch.

The aesthetics are amazing. Every single item on it, I love, from the aeroscreen to the Jäger speedo, to the totally useless brass fire extinguisher, to the cycle wings, to the leather-bound bonding of the body, to the huge Monza filler cap, to the pheasant, which perches, for no reason at all, on the front of the radiator, to the mega P100 lights.

The noise that she makes when she is running is something that I can't live without. It's this beautiful purring growl.

I love every single part of it, but it's how those parts come together that make it, for my money, the coolest little car of its ilk I've ever seen.

She's got huge racing history, and the way to keep a car like this going, and to add value to it (although I know I will never sell it), is to keep racing her. So I compete at Prescot and I come last, but in the hands of a decent driver, she could get right up the board.

I sit in there probably three times a week with a cup of tea in the morning, just for no reason other than to be with her, you know. That's what I do. Janie thinks I'm mad.

Chapter 46

One thing I would definitely say if you're planning an international motorcycle adventure for the first time is don't start with Russia.

The worst way you can pick a motorbike odyssey is to look at a map and go, 'Ooh. That looks nice.' But of course, that's how everyone does it – including me and Hamish when we are making *World's Greatest Motorcycle Rides*. The whole ethos of the show, for twenty-three series, has always been: pick a route that you can do in two to three weeks. We leave going round the world to Charlie Boorman and Ewan McGregor because I reckon most people can't afford to do that and, if they did, they would come back skint and unemployed. *World's Greatest* has always been about marrying up a natural passion for adventure motorcycling with the mundane reality of having a job, kids and a mortgage.

So three weeks is the upper limit. And that means, as Napoleon might have told the Hell's Angels: Don't Do Russia.

The trouble is, on the map, it all looks groovy. St Petersburg to Moscow. Five hundred miles east. But Hamish – yes I blame him totally for this – decided that instead of doing that, we would go north, and then come back down again, like a triangle, to make it more interesting.

It was 2000 miles of fucking interesting.

I thought – from watching Charlie Boorman and Ewan McGregor, I must admit – that Russia was basically ok until you got east of Moscow.

I was keen on using a Harley, but then it worked out that we couldn't actually get one into Russia in that time frame. So we rang KTM and asked: 'Any chance of a 990?'

They went, 'Yeah, sure,' but then they rang back and said, 'Sorry. The Mafia won't let it in.'

So I had no bike, and although I really, really didn't want to use the same bikes that Charlie and Euan had (a GS1200) and generally, I wouldn't be seen dead on one of those, there was no alternative.

Just like any other punters, we rented one and it was delivered to the hotel in St Petersburg.

We spent two or three days doing St Petersburg. The sun was shining, the buildings were glorious, Hamish was behaving himself and the bike was . . . well, it was actually ok, this GS1200. And I was thinking, This trip's going to be an absolute belter.

Then, the morning comes to clear off, and we leave St Petersburg, heading north. I'm doing 75 miles an hour, cruising on this beautiful dual carriageway A-road, and I crank the bike into a bend, come round it . . . and the road stops. It just stops. One moment it's a proper, big, wide A-road, the next it's gravel and mud.

I slam on the brakes and get off the bike and go, 'Hamish, you knob, what are you taking us down here for, man? We must have taken a wrong turn.'

He checks his map and goes, 'No, mate, this is the A-road.'

I suddenly learned that if Russia was going to invade Europe, they wouldn't be able to do it very quickly because they haven't got any roads.

So I'm standing there cursing Hamish, having a vape and it starts to rain.

And it doesn't stop raining for three weeks.

I get back on the bike and drive through mud, rubble and potholes for the next 2000 miles, with juggernauts coming towards me in the middle of the road, as they're avoiding the potholes too.

We did get completely lost on multiple occasions, as we always do. (I love it when people go, 'Oh, it's all right for you, Henry. You've got a camera crew with you, and on your budget, you could get a helicopter to take you out of there.' Er, no.) There've been many times – in Australia, America, South Lapland or Serbia – where we have genuinely been in big trouble – no sat nav and maps which don't correlate to the real world.

And in most other places that's all right; it's maybe even part of the fun. But the difference with Russia is it just feels so lawless. You've got a nice bike, you've got a nice Discovery as a camera truck and you feel you're a sitting duck for Olav to materialize with an AK and come over all bald with you.

You feel constantly threatened in Russia.

We were going to supper one evening and three guys just appeared with chrome-plated Kalashnikovs and flak jackets coming down the fire exit towards us. Everyone's driving round in 500 SLs with blacked-out windows. It seems that all Russians are bald and wear shades. No one smiles at you. And obviously, you can't speak the lingo.

So you feel very alienated and nervous most of the time in Russia, especially if you are someone like me who believes that they don't fit in with society anyway.

When you do get tarmac in Russia, there's a 3-foot-wide diesel slick in the middle of the road the whole way because everyone's running knackered old lorries, spewing out diesel everywhere; so even on the best road, you have probably 6–10 feet of tarmac that's ok. If you slip off that, you're in the bushes, mate, and no one wants to go to a Russian hospital.

Another problem with Russia is that no one appears to have passed their driving test. They've bought it, and now they're learning on the job.

Time and time again I'd be going pretty quick and I'd be overtaking a car, and over my shoulder comes some geezer overtaking me.

I'm on a GS1200 and Hamish is in a Discovery, and we can easily do 100 miles an hour. These dudes are in beaten-up Škodas, and they're pinning it; they're just lunatics. And there's no insurance. You just give the coppers $100 and they're sweet as a nut. That's why they pull you.

It's pretty scary. In certain situations, in places like Russia, you genuinely believe that you may not come out of this.

The hotels out in the country are insane. Supper? You just wait at an empty table and they bring you some slurry. And that's it.

One time, after we had finished eating, the bloke came up and he went, 'Do you want pudding? Do you want dessert?'

I went, 'Yeah, cheers.'

'Ok.'

And off he went, and brought us back three Ferrero Rocher chocolates. One each. The ambassador is really fucking spoiling us!

Russia is a frontier country, so while it can seem chaotic to a visitor, it runs to its own rules. And the number-one rule is: you can get anything if you've got the money. If you ain't got the money, you are stuffed.

When you go into a regional town, as you get into it, the roads get progressively worse, until, in the middle, the roads are mud, with gigantic Russian potholes; they are so big that if you drop your front tyre into one of them, you won't get out. And the reason they are so bad is because the money's generally been used for something else, such as a penthouse in Chelsea.

Meeting the Russian biker gangs was cool though. I met the black-bear motorcycle club. They wear black waistcoats made out of bearskin, and they ride crazy chops. They're hardcore bastards – but so damned nice as well.

They had this beautiful but dilapidated townhouse in the middle of the poshest part of Yaroslavl as their club-house, with a bar and a nightclub and all that kind of stuff. They took me down to this place they had on an industrial estate – a massive area of about 5 acres behind mega gates that was theirs – their play area for riding bikes and messing about.

I just called everyone 'Sir' and smiled a lot.

*

After three weeks of rain and not falling off, all we had left to do was to drive into Moscow. A local guy who's helping us goes, 'Don't go to Moscow today.'

'What do you mean, Danny?'

He goes, 'We'll go in Sunday morning, and we only go on this route.'

'Why's that?'

'Because that's our only chance of not getting gridlocked.'

It doesn't work. Sunday morning comes and we do 80 miles in five and a half hours in the pissing rain.

What's fascinating is that we're all stuck in the three lanes of the normal carriageway, going into Moscow, but the hard shoulder is streaming with tough, bald people in Audis driving along like lunatics in brand-new motors. And then there's a fifth lane, which is the grass, beyond the hard shoulder, full of bald people in Range Rovers.

That sums up Russia's class structure.

The GS1200 was actually exactly the right bike for that trip. Without a bike like that, Russia is impregnable. If we had got that Harley in, I would have got as far as 50 miles out of St Petersburg and then it would have been time to go back there to lick our wounds and think again.

It was a hire bike, so it was total shit in one way, but it kept on going. And it's a dual-sport bike, so it can do off-road and on-road, and the great thing about that is you can do 120 miles an hour when you get some tarmac, or you can do 50–70 miles an hour on dirt with total confidence.

I've done a lot of dirt riding doing *World's Greatest Motorcycle Rides*, and I've done a lot of training now.

I'd been a road rider for forty years, and, as a road rider, the one thing you know is that gravel will kill you. Because if you go into a corner and there's gravel all over the road, your front wheel washes out, your rear wheel slides and you're throwing yourself at the countryside.

So when some geezer tells you to pin it down a gravel road it's slightly alarming. You have to stand up on the pegs, which helps to put as much weight on the front tyre as possible and then you just go for it, trusting your sixth sense is going to guide you. You never look at the rock/tree/hole you're trying to avoid, or you will smack straight into it.

The way to survive on dirt is to go as quick as possible within your abilities. The more power you put down, the more grip the knobbly tyres have, and if you can imagine a really rutted road, what you want to be doing is 50–60 miles an hour, so that you are bouncing over the bumps, flying over the top, only hitting one out of four, rather than every single one.

But you've got to pin it for it to come together, and then you suddenly get it.

The thing that Russia showed me was that if you're setting off on an adventure, pick wisely. Don't pick something on the basis that it sounds good in the pub. Riding Russia is incredibly taxing, so you've got to be experienced. You've got to be a good off-road rider, and you've got to know how to handle a bike with your eyes closed because, frankly, that's the least of your worries. There's so much other shit to deal with.

If you're still worrying about how to ride off-road, and a juggernaut's coming towards you, and it's pissing with rain, and you're on the oil slick, and your sleeping bag – which you reckon is well cool to have on the back – starts to slip off and gets caught in your rear wheel, you're in all kinds of shit. You'll be dead within a hundred miles, when what you should be doing is riding in Croatia and having a lovely time.

Manage your expectations to your capabilities and you'll have a blast.

The reward of Russia is the opportunity to immerse yourself in a culture that is so unbelievably different to ours. Everyone out in the sticks has one priority: staying alive. They are self-sufficient in the extreme: there are no roadside-assistance services in Russia, but there are inspection pits built into the side of the road every so often.

Russia is basically shit. Medical care is shit, the roads are shit, shops are shit, food's shit, the weather's shit. Everything's shit. But they seem to be able to carry on and look for the good things in life.

If you know what you are doing and you go and do Russia as three or four riders of dual-sport bikes, you'll either come back a closer, tighter community of people, or you'll come back on different planes or in boxes.

You'll certainly find out who your mates are, and what you and they are really made of.

So if you want a true adventure, ride in Russia. If you want to nearly die every three quarters of an hour, go to Russia.

If you want to say, 3000 miles later, 'I survived it' – go to Russia.

Chapter 47

As someone who successfully avoided needles as a heroin addict in the 80s, it's rather ironic, to say the least, that I now rely on regular injections to keep me alive – or at least to keep up an acceptable intake of cherry Bakewells.

Strange things happen to you in life, don't they?

Just when you think it's all going rather well, it all goes horribly wrong.

That's what happened with me and diabetes.

I've always thought of myself as a thin person, but for some reason, in my late forties, I became quite fat.

It didn't just happen. I really got heavily involved in sugar. I guess I was missing the smack deep down inside somewhere; you definitely do swap around addictions as a sober addict, but as long as it ain't drugs or drink you've got a hope.

Anyway, thanks to my fondness for sugar, I was about 16 stone around 2002. Prior to that I'd always been about 12 stone, then I suddenly put on weight because I had my office in London, I was stressed out of my skull, I was drinking a lot of cappuccinos with two sugars, I'd drink about six or seven cans of fat Coke a day and I'd supplement that with quite a lot of chocolate and about two or three packs of extra-strong mints.

Then, I went to Italy to direct a commercial for Baxi Boilers – yeah, all glamour, this job – and I felt very unusual.

But I am a hypochondriac, so there's never a day that goes by without an ailment of some description. Still, I found myself drinking so much water. I was insanely thirsty on the plane on the way home, and I could not quench my thirst at all.

I emptied the plane of soft drinks, all of which were obviously filled with sugar, which made it even worse.

So I got off the plane feeling like a barrel full of carbonated water, and this went on for about a week afterwards. I was feeling more and more unusual until, eventually, I Googled it and diagnosed myself with diabetes.

Diabetes scared the shit out of me. When I was a kid, up in Norfolk, our dog, Lulu, got diabetes. We had to inject her every day and then she'd pass out and have fits and it was all pretty scary.

So I went to my doctor and I said, 'Look, mate, no really, I feel unusual. I can't quench my thirst. I think I've got diabetes.'

And he said, 'Oh don't be so bloody stupid. Why would you have diabetes?'

'Well, I don't know really, but I think I have.'

'Ok,' he went, 'well, look, pee on this stick.'

I came back in the room, he looked at the stick and he went, 'Fuck me, you have!'

That was his diagnosis.

He asked, 'Shall we go and have a snout and talk about it outside?'

So we went out and had a fag together – and that was the start of me having diabetes.

I went to see a diabetes specialist and he said, 'Well you're diabetic. From now on, you're not to smoke, you're not to eat sugar and you are to change your life.'

I looked at him and thought, You are a prick. You've got no idea how to handle people like me. I can sort it out myself, thanks, mate.

Great reaction, right?

To cut a long story short, all my organs were all right, but for some reason I got diabetes. To this day, I don't think they know whether it's type 2 or type 1 – type 1 being genetic and type 2 being late-onset, fat-related diabetes. They think it's type 1, but there's no one in my family with it, so it might just be extra-strong-mint-related fattery or an after effect of the heroin. Or maybe it was the full-fat Coke that pushed me over the edge.

Anyway, my body went into meltdown and started eating itself. I went down to 10 stone from 16 in about six weeks. I went round the various specialists again and they all said, 'Look, Henry, if you want to lead a normal life, you need to inject.'

I couldn't believe it! I was so proud of never injecting when I was using.

So this woman turned up with an orange and a syringe to teach me how to inject. I was like, 'Yeah, I know a few people who could have used your advice in 1989, babe.'

I've had diabetes for fifteen years now, from completely out of the blue. Emotionally, it's incredible how shit like that changes your life. It's made me aware that I'm vulnerable.

Up to 2003, I was this geezer who'd jump off cliffs, do underwater diving, ride like a nutter, I didn't give a fuck. Because I'm a hypochondriac, I didn't think I was invincible – but I did think that I could get to grips with most things. But when you have your first hypo, you understand that you actually are fallible.

Like a lot of people with chronic diseases who have to adapt their lives to deal with it, I was really floundering emotionally in the first few years.

Everyone was saying, 'Oh, Henry, you've got to give up everything. You've got to know exactly what you're going to have for lunch, you've got to really control your routine to control your diabetes.'

Well, I made a decision early on that I was going to control my diabetes as best I could, come hell or high water, but that it was not going to affect how I lived my life.

I travel all over the world, I ride bikes all the time and I have the craziest routine ever.

But what I do now is to build in an understanding – mentally, spiritually and physically – of how to operate with diabetes, and how I can lead a normal life. That means telling everyone around me that I'm diabetic. And it means that whether it's *World's Greatest Motorcycle Rides* or a land speed attempt or going live on TV, I have to have sugars right before I do it. Or I'll be filming, and I'll say to the crew, 'Lads, I've got to go lie in a bush for ten minutes', and I'll have a bag of jelly babies because I'm having a bit of a sugar low.

Now, my long-term sugars seem very good when I go for my check-ups, which I am meticulous about. I am also meticulous with my check-ups, my testing and my sugar control, but I know a lot of people who aren't. They bury their heads in the sand. And consequently, they have a lot of problems.

It's weird that for such a medically well-understood disease there are an awful lot of diabetics out there who don't seem to understand what they've got. I've met some who don't know what they're doing by taking insulin. They don't know that if you are diabetic, that means your body's packed up making insulin, so you need to put it in if you have anything sugary. They don't understand that – so what hope is there?

I'm no doctor, but if you respect the disease, and you do your utmost to control it, then I think you've really got a good chance at leading a normal life. People are scared by what they hear about it, and the worst thing you can do is go on the internet and see how people's feet have fallen off and shit. That's through really bad sugar control over many years.

Diabetes has been a massive life-changer for me. I wouldn't have got through it without the wife and the people I work with. Probably, at the end of the day, it will kill me, but I refuse to let it kill my soul. And I think that's the key thing about it.

Like everything in life, really, it's up to you what you make out of it.

Your destiny is controlled by you, and if you blank it and put it under the carpet and all that kind of caper, then you're fucked.

It took me about two or three years to accept at a gut level that I've got it. Every time I go to the doctor, they say there'll be a cure in three years. I'm like, 'No. There won't be.'

Diabetes was a real leveller because I realized that I was vulnerable.

Not drinking helps. If you drink and are diabetic, you've got more of an issue because you have no idea how much sugar's in that glass of Sauvignon Blanc, whereas I kind of know how much sugar's in a cherry Bakewell.

And if I want a cherry Bakewell, then I'm going to have one, and adjust my insulin accordingly. Put a little bit more in to cope with it. But I have to be sensible.

I have to admit I love sugar. My favourite things in the world are sherbet fountains. You know, what would you rather have? A knickerbocker glory or some kale soup? Well, for me I'd have a knickerbocker glory all day long. Janie tries desperately to get me to eat healthy food, and I do, but if she gives me one more broccoli stalk, I'll divorce her. Broccoli has got to be food for aliens. How can anyone think that stuff is edible? It smells of shit and it tastes of diluted shit. And what's all this quinoa stuff? I genuinely don't understand it, you know. Rocket? Rocket was a weed on French roads.

Sugar's one of the greatest things in the world. But it's like everything that is absolutely wonderful in life – you've got to be very careful how much you take.

So I am. And I am not at the same time. It's my life, this is how I want to live it and the diabetes can come along for the ride. That's the way I see it.

I might knock five years off myself by doing that, but I've knocked so many five years off myself already, I should have died in 2007.

When you're diagnosed with a chronic disease like diabetes, you really feel winded at first.

There's then a period of acceptance that you need to go through.

And then it's incredible how adaptable you discover you are.

You learn how to cope with shit that's been thrown at you in life and you just look for the positive things in it. And for me, the positive thing about diabetes is that I can share my story with people who've just got it. They're terrified and I get to say to them, 'It's ok, mate. There is life after diabetes. There is great life even with diabetes. And fuck anyone who tells you otherwise.

Duo Petrol Can

The duo petrol cans were 2-gallon cans back in the 1920s. They were two cans in one, so you would go and buy your petrol, but they also had a can within the can where you'd put your oil. So you got a cylindrical can within the square 2-gallon one because an awful lot of the vehicles in those days were total-loss oil systems, meaning that once the oil had lubricated the engine, it just pissed out onto the ground, so you'd have to refill the oil as much as you filled the petrol. My little duo can is something that I cherish massively because it's in really good nick and it's just the loveliest thing to behold. All I've done is polish the brass cap and give it a clean. But just to look at that, man. I'm just a saddo who sits in my shed, drinks tea and looks at that can, imagining what it's seen in this life.

And I love that. That's what history's all about, isn't it? And it also embodies this whole concept that automotive memorabilia is the new antiques because it's so relevant to the modern day. You look at a duo petrol can and you are looking at the technology which basically drove the motorized revolution of the 20s (long after the first petrol pump arrived at Brooklands race track in 1908). These petrol cans instigated pop and modern-day culture. They are pure automotive history. So you've got to own some of the best of those, haven't you?

Chapter 48

Like a lot of motorbike riders, I've always been obsessed with Steve McQueen, the motorcycling movie star, and I always dreamed of maybe one day making a film about him. And last year that dream came true. I got to make two fims about McQueen and his love of bikes for ITV – happy fucking days! Ever since I was really young, I've idolized that guy because I absolutely believed that here was a man who was perceived to be the king of cool and actually really was just that. We'll probably never have another guy like him – just like we won't have The Beatles or the Stones – because he came from a time in pop culture when icons were made. Now, icons are made every twenty minutes and it's not quite the same.

So Steve McQueen, to me, was an icon. I wanted to find out much more about him. He only lived till he was fifty and, in that time, he fulfilled a huge amount of what I and so many other bikers aspire to and want to do.

The bare bones of his story are remarkable enough. He had a totally dysfunctional upbringing: his mother had a million partners and all that kind of stuff, and he was brought up on the wrong side of the tracks. After a really stormy and abusive childhood, he ended up at the reform school in Los Angeles, for what they called juvenile delinquents. He then left that place, went into the military, wound up in New York and bought himself an Indian motorcycle – because motorcycles, to him, were where it was at.

He embodied everything that I yearned to have when I was younger, which was, 'Fuck you, fuck the world. I'm doing my thing.'

He came from the school of hard knocks. He was good-looking, but other than that he had no leg up. Still, he managed to cobble together enough wages to buy his motorcycle. (One of his first girlfriends said, 'It's either me or the bike'. He dumped her.)

He went to art school and then ended up in Los Angeles at stage school. He said the only reason he wanted to get in there was because there were chicks there.

Anyway, he went, found out that he was pretty good and got a part in the TV series *Dead or Alive*. And that was his break.

When he got his first big pay cheque, he rode out one day in LA to find Bud Ekins, a legendary stuntman who later did the stunts in *The Great Escape*. Bud had a Triumph dealership in Sherman Oaks in LA and Steve turned up there one day to meet the man and then, later, the whole community of people within motorcycling – and that was the one community where he could be himself. Those people were his real friends. Wives came and went, but Bud Ekins, Bobby Foxworth, Dave Ekins, Cliff Coleman – all those people who went out desert racing – they never let Steve McQueen down.

Even when he rejected Hollywood and went off with Ali McGraw, out into the deserts, he did that on a motorcycle.

Now he is known for his cars, and quite rightly so, but at the end of the day, cars were the things that let him down. Cars gave him the nightmare that was the making of the movie *Le Mans*. But the motorcycles never let him down. Motorcycles made him an icon through the jump on *The Great Escape*. Of course, he didn't do that stunt – he would have loved to but the studio wouldn't allow it. Bud Ekins did that jump. For him.

Steve McQueen insisted that a motorcycle should feature in his escape. On the script it just says: 'motorcycle sequence refer McQueen.'

So he came up with this idea that he would nick a motorcycle from the Germans, be chased by them and then be impeded by a load of tank traps and a big wire fence. And he would jump over it.

That was basically the gig and that's what he wanted to do.

The studios were, of course, not about to sign off on him doing a stunt like that. He could easily have broken an arm and been unable to finish the movie.

So he enlisted the help of Ekins. And he jumped a TR6 Triumph 13 feet.

That doesn't sound much if you're running a motocross bike today, you know, but with an old bike it was. And there was really only one person who could do that and that was Bud Ekins. He only had one attempt and he pulled it off.

McQueen had a reputation for hating any stuntman being on set at the same time as him. If the stuntman was doubling him, and wearing the same clothes as he was wearing on set, McQueen would always go away and change.

But with that stunt, he publicly said, 'It was Bud Ekins, who did it not me.' That completely went against the grain of how he operated.

Some other interesting little things about that jump: that motorcycle was a TR6 Triumph, painted in green. And it was built in 1962; that's when it was released. Well, hang on a sec – Steve McQueen was running from the Germans in 1942. And he nicked a British bike off them when it should have been a German one. And the brief was to paint it green for Bud Ekins because it was a military bike – but actually all the German bikes were grey.

So basically, Bud goes and does this jump on a 1962 British bike when he's a German, in Germany, and no one gives a toss except me.

I found out from the people who worked with him on movies that McQueen was generally a very difficult person to work with. He was a control freak. He also was a perfectionist and he did not suffer anyone telling him how to do things.

McQueen was a bad boy and he had always been a bad boy, a cool bad boy and a guy who had been through the school of hard knocks. If he was playing a good guy, there would be something slightly sinister about him on screen. But strangely, if he was playing a bad guy, there was something really endearing about him. And I believe you can only get that in a movie as an actor if you've actually been through those hard knocks and understand how to manipulate or how to fight to get your way – because the camera can see it.

Having made those two films and delved into his life, I'm convinced McQueen was only happy when he was racing or riding.

Just as a motorcycle frees people from their mundane

lives, motorcycling freed Steve McQueen from the Hollywood studios which dictated his life and he despised. So it doesn't matter whether you are a dustman who rides a motorcycle for escapism or you're one of the most famous Hollywood actors who scorns the bullshit fakery of the executives and world around you; motorcycling gives you the freedom to be whoever you are.

Chapter 49

If you have yourself a heroin addiction, when you stop the heroin, it's not like you are just going to be able to cruise on through the rest of your life as a normal, regular person. Most of us sober addicts still have the same addictive personality after we've got over the drugs.

Addiction is the issue; heroin, alcohol, cigarettes and buying vast quantities of vintage motorbikes – well, they are just the symptoms.

So you can get off the heroin and learn all about why you shouldn't be taking mood-altering chemicals and never touch them again, but that doesn't get you away from the fact that you're a raving nutbar, which is probably why you took smack in the first place.

The compulsive, obsessive and addictive personality that I clearly always had still manifests itself, but it's controllable to a degree. Part of the secret to a successful recovery is to embrace that reality and try to harness those characteristics into something productive.

For me, that's my work.

I am completely and totally a workaholic.

I work twelve or fourteen hours a day, seven days a week. I take one holiday a year, and I spend most of it sending emails.

It's not that I don't enjoy holidays; it's just I don't really see the point because I live, breathe and shit my work, to the point where it ain't work, it's just my life. Even when I'm watching the kids at a cricket match (and I do all that stuff and I love it), I'm still working – because I might see the ride-on lawnmower and suddenly have an amazing idea for a new episode of *Find It, Fix It, Flog It*.

Loads of people ring me up for a get together and ask, 'What time do you finish normally?'

I always say, 'I don't finish. I've never finished.'

I was, I think, very fucking lucky to have ambition, even in the depths of my addiction. As I have said, it helped motivate me to get sober in the early days. I have been clean from drugs and alcohol for thirty years, and ambition has definitely become the driving force in my life since then.

But it's not ambition the way most people see it. I don't want to be a multimillionaire and have yachts. I mean, yeah, I need enough money to collect my vehicles, but the real addiction of ambition for me is to prove to myself that I was worth it.

I don't need to prove that to anyone else.

People say to me, 'What's your end goal?'

Well I'm living my end goal every day: doing my shows, talking shit to people, going out on the bike, presenting six different TV series and writing this book.

That's all I really ever wanted, to prove to myself that I actually could give something back. And if I make people laugh a little bit, and I make people go, 'Fuck me, I never knew you could restore that,' or, 'Fucking hell, Henry, that git, is riding across Australia in 45-degree heat, that's funny,' then I've done my job.

I don't want to be on *Have I Got News for You?*. I don't want to do any bubble-gum celebrity Rob Brydon-type shit, you know. I'm just me and I'm just delighted that I've got to write a book about all the stuff that makes me tick.

I don't think I am a workaholic because I'm avoiding deeper issues (I've done all that therapy) but because, through my work, I'm immersing myself in my reason to live.

I can't get enough of it. That's why I get up at six o'clock every morning and bust my arse all day. I'm satisfied by it and I love it. And I love the people who do it with me. The day I wake up and think, 'Oh, fuck. I've got to restore a motorbike today,' then I'm going to hang up my helmet.

But that ain't going to happen. Because if it was, it would have done so by now.

My Beard

I do notice that most shed dwellers and motorcyclists have beards. This is partly down to the individualism – although now that all the hipsters are growing them, and so is Prince Harry, beards are not quite as rebellious as they once were.

But facial hair does have its benefits on a motorcycle. It does actually keep you warm, but again you can catch an awful lot of things in the summer in your beard that you will only discover when you shower.

Obviously, the beard is an image. And I personally believe that if you can grow one, it's definitely worth it.

I like facial hair on a man. I think the beard immediately says something. It says, 'I'm an individual; I'm different.'

A beard goes well with the long hair, which is, practically speaking, a nightmare. It gets knotted. It gets stuck in the helmet. It comes down over your eyes sometimes. But the great thing about long hair and a beard is that if you suddenly don't want to be into biking any more, you can go to the barber.

So I would suggest before you cover yourself in paint or tattoos, grow a beard and see how you go from there. Because it could be a kind of transient moment.

Chapter 50

Part of my workaholism is related to the knowledge that one day I'll wake up and it will all be over, the phone will stop ringing and I'll just toddle off to my shed with a pack of ginger nuts and a mug of tea and figure out what I need to sell first.

And I won't be one of those people who say, 'Oh, I never thought that would ever happen to me,' because in TV it's always just a question of when.

And I know everything is going to happen to me.

That's my approach to life. I don't think I'm going to dodge the bullet. I'm going to stand up and take it square in the fucking head, man.

I sometimes think I don't believe in me as much as some other people – Hamish, Sam and Guy spring to mind – do.

Deep down, I think an awful lot of people are like that.

I find it hard to accept compliments. When someone says, 'Henry, that was such a great show,' I thank them profusely, but it's taken me probably fifteen years, minimum, to actually accept that when someone is saying that to me, they perhaps really mean it.

I think it's because I don't want people to think I'm arrogant. I've met so many arrogant people in this game; people who don't turn up on time and then don't apologise. I fucking hate that. And I have sat there trying to direct someone in a crappy commercial and they've been demanding grilled sea bass in the middle of a field. Who do you think you are, mate?

I don't understand how people get to that mentality in life, where they genuinely believe it's ok to be shouting and screaming at people just because they are deemed lesser than them in some bullshit pecking order.

When I finish a shoot with a crew I don't know, I go round, I shake everyone by the hand and I thank everybody, because I know what it's like to be at the bottom and I'll never forget that.

I don't believe being arrogant about being relatively good at something does you any favours at all. Being humble, that's what makes you strive on and keep taking on your own personal demons. And that's what I do, day in and day out.

I don't want to read the news.

I don't want to present the lottery.

I don't want to go on studio shows.

I just want to be me in a shed and going off around the place, which is, basically, what I do.

Shed and Buried instigated a small institution because we are now doing *Junk and Disorderly* for ITV, *The History of Motorcycles* and *The Motorbike Show* for ITV4 and *Find It, Fix It, Flog It* for Channel 4, and *Find It, Fix It, Drive It* for More4 and Channel 4.

I'm still doing *World's Greatest Motorcycle Rides* and I've just done a railway restoration series for Channel 4 with Peter Snow. A fucking icon of a man.

I just want people to join me in the love and passion that I have not only for motorcycles, but also for the restoration of all kinds of classic vehicles and that joyous thing: British engineering.

My big dream now is to do the history of automotive Britain and industrial Britain.

Imagine that. I want to restore steam locomotives. I want to restore steam-traction engines. I want to restore more and more motorcycles. I want to restore pick-ups from the 40s. I want to restore drag bikes. I want to restore anything that's quirky and individual.

I've got my little house, got my long-suffering wife, my two little men, my collection of vehicles and a career presenting shows. Now, if that continues till I drop dead, then I'm the happiest man who's still alive until I'm not.

But if we are really talking do-anything-you-want, have-three-wishes stuff, then there is one other thing I want to do.

I want to make one more movie – just to prove I can.

Because *Mad Dogs*, still to this day, twenty-four years on – it still hurts me, if I'm really honest.

What hurts me most is the thought of the opportunity I spanked, and why I spanked it; because I didn't know what I was doing. I was a rookie, you know, and I was relying on other people who were rookies, and so, what hope was there for *Mad Dogs*?

I do still believe, if I've got the bollocks, I've got a movie left in me.

I wrote a script when I finished *Mad Dogs* to try to encapsulate my feelings as a result of that experience – the loneliness, the isolation and the feeling of being not heard – and I came up with a script for a movie called *Danny*. But when everything blew up financially with the company, I didn't then have the ability to make my 'comeback movie' – so *Danny*'s still waiting.

To try to encapsulate it like you have to do in LA, it's *Billy Elliot* with guns. But in a bit more detail, it's about a guy called Danny whose alter ego is John Travolta in *Saturday Night Fever*. Danny is brought up in a care home in Blackpool, while his elder brother, who's the local disco-dancing champion, is serving two years in prison for a bungled robbery. Danny goes out and gets pissed, and he looks in a cinema memorabilia shop where John Travolta comes to him – a John Travolta cutout comes to him – and says, 'Danny, you can have the suit now. I got a job on *Pulp Fiction*.'

So Danny gets a suit made by his carer, and it's all about disco dancing in horizontal rain on Blackpool pier, just trying to get through life. That's what it's about.

I showed it to an agency in Los Angeles and when they read the script, they said half of it is genius and half of it is shit. Trouble is, they didn't tell me which parts were genius and which parts were shit.

So that's the future. That and to grow old disgracefully with my wife. Just as long as I never have to fucking retire and wait to die, I'll be all right.

Thank God, I have freedom. I have the freedom to tell the world and everyone else to sod off, if I want to – which I don't, today, but there's always that option.

I sound just like my dad, don't I? Funny that.

My freedom is to only work with people I want to work with. Everyone who works with me or for me is a top geezer or lady and if anyone gets in here who I don't like, they're gone, because they won't want to be here, anyway.

My freedom is to tell some TV executive who asks me to send them a synopsis of *World's Greatest Motorcycle Rides* to fuck off and watch a few.

My freedom is self-respect.

My freedom is that I believe I haven't sold out.

My freedom is that I believe in my own little way I've got integrity.

My freedom is that I'm no one's puppet.

And that's a freedom that I'll never let go of.

Chapter 51

Well, look, that's nearly me done. If you made it this far, thank you so much, really, genuinely, from the bottom of my heart, for reading this. It means so much to me to have had the opportunity to write it.

Before I go, I just want to say one more thing about drugs and addiction, because it's an issue that goes to the very heart of my story, and it affects so many bikers and their families, and I know how bleak it can all look when you are in it.

I firmly believe, and I hope my story in some tiny way shows, that most addicts have a tremendous amount to offer, if you can just get off the drugs.

I mean, it's amazing, really, when you stop to think about it, what junkies manage to achieve on a daily basis. These people are waking up penniless in a sleeping bag on the street at seven in the morning and somehow managing to get £25 together to score a quarter of a gram by lunchtime.

Now, obviously I don't condone how they get that cash together. But, at the same time, please don't tell me that they are a bunch of thick, inconsequential idiots with no drive or ability.

So I really feel very strongly that addiction is a thing that we need to learn to channel in the right way, and it's in society's interests to help people who can't help themselves to do that.

When we don't, we all pay the price.

I'd love to do a TV show where I take a dirty dozen of the nastiest junkies in the UK, clean them out and train them up to take aid to war zones. I mean, obviously it will never happen because the suits would say it's exploitative and you can't put junkies on TV. But the point is, when other people are relying on you for their lives, you see what you are really made of, and most junkies I knew were made of pretty stern stuff.

Fundamentally, I know how lucky I was to get clean, and the fact I was educated and had a good job and a somewhat supportive family really helped, but just as I believe that no one in society should be disregarded because of their background, then don't tell me that because my great-great-great-great-uncle was Gladstone I should have known better.

Maybe I was born with a silver spoon in my mouth, but that's irrelevant. Addiction is truly classless. When you're in cold turkey, it doesn't make any difference where you went to fucking school, mate.

It's terrible the way addicts are treated. They are still being put in prison for no reason.

If you've murdered someone or robbed a house, you've got to do your time, and who gives a monkey's if you were high at the time, but addicts getting done for possession and being put in prison?

Why?

That's where you get *more* drugs.

Society's approach to people with addiction problems is to cast them out, which is so short-sighted because if you can actually redirect that addictive spirit into something positive, then it's a win–win for society and for the individual.

Society needs us. Humanity needs us.

Really? Well, yes. Please don't tell me that Van Gogh was a normal person. Don't tell me that Jimi Hendrix was a normal person. The list of people who were addicts and then channelled their addiction into something very productive is a long one

I know, deep down, I am still a junkie, just one who hasn't used for a fair bit – because I still feel on some days that I absolutely do not fit into this society that I live in. I still sometimes feel I don't know what life is all about, why we're doing any of this.

In the blink of an eye, I'll be lying on my deathbed (and so will you – because, as previously noted, none of us gets out of here alive), and I'll be in my pyjamas, probably, or on a drip or whatever, going in and out of consciousness. You know, faint smell of pee, hum of machines. And at that moment, would I be thinking about my yacht in the Maldives if I had one?

No.

I'd be thinking about what everyone thinks about: my needs, my survival and how I have treated my family.

Have I lived my life on my own terms, how I wanted to live it?

Have I got the most out of it?

Have I taken care of those I love and who have been decent enough to love me?

Life is about contentment and peace of mind. It's about

being whole as a person, and creating my own little world, however small that world may be. A world that is a safe place for me and my family.

So you know, when I'm dying of heart disease or cancer or whatever it is, all that matters is that there are a few people there with me who love me.

It makes me think of my father. One thing he always said to me, was, 'Do what the fuck you want, Henry, as long as it doesn't hurt anyone else.'

Not a bad rule for life, eh?

With deepest thanks to those who've supported me along the way:

Janie & The Boys, Vivien Cole, Major Denis Cole, David & Pam Coombes, Anna & Ashley Coombes, Martha & Robbie Coombes, Tom Sykes, Hamish Rieck, Jonathan Conway, Guy (Skid) Willison, Jo Colson, Steve Back, Uncle Dick Redbeard, Sebastian Rich, Ben Tinsley, Richard Milner, Annabelle Norton, Tommy Clarke, Jon Wood, Sylvia & Fred Tidy Harris, Deaglan Bayliss, Mick Conefrey, Bumble, Rick Aplin, Rupert & Torica Back, Paul Bader, Emma Barker, Amanda Barker, Bear, Tamara Beckwith, Alice Beer, Zai Bennett, Henry & Kathy Birtles, Nanna & Ziggi Bollason, Ed Booth, Johnny Boscawen, Johnny Boston, Claire Bosworth, Luke Brackenbury, Vincent Browett, Anne & Rob Burchell, Amanda Byram, William Campbell, Caprice, Alan Cathcart, Gabe Chauveau, Mark & Gerry Chauveau, Martin Chisholm, John Claridge, Luke Clayden, Steve Coates, Emma Collins, Spencer & Tish Cooper, Nikki Cooper, Richard Cox, Alan & Caroline Crisp, Charlie & Anna Crossley-Cooke, Tim & Suzanne Dams, Mike Day, Charles Dean, Henry Dent Brocklehurst, Steve Earle, Julie Anne Edwards, Patrick Edwards, Anna & Ali Ekin, The Ekins Family, Josh Elliot, Leah Foley, Patrick & Ferrylyn Folkes, Jeff Ford, Bobby Foxworth, Tim Frewer, Steve Fright, Pip Froud, Stuart Garner, Ken German, Jamie Gidlow-Jackson, Charlie Gladstone, Louise Goodman, Nicki Gottlieb, Charlie Grainger, Alan Greenspan, Sam Hardy, Andy and Carol Harris, Simon Hawkins, Jacqueline Hewer, Reggie Heyworth, Caryn & Jerry Hibbert, Chris and Mel Hicks, Simon Hilton, John & Karen Holloway, Ed Howard, Diana Howie, Elizabeth Hurley, Katie Hurley, Tony Hutchinson, Invercargill A&E,